The Earth Turns

A Book of Poetry
By Karen Melander-Magoon

ISBN-978-1-7355892-1-3

Curious Muse Press
San Francisco

Preface

In response to my book of poetry, A Year of Anguish, A Time for Miracles, I continue seeking better understanding of our world through poetry.

I want to thank my friends and family and all in my life who have inspired and guided me through this year with their thoughts and love.

As I write this, my page is flashed with an announcement of more Covid cases and deaths. Our world is still in pain.

In contrast to A Year of Anguish, these poems reach back as far as 2013. They range from outrage to whimsy and humor, they touch on science and history, but above all on our own human condition and our hopes for the future. They also include the lyrics to several of my songs.

I hope this poetry will give us all a new sense of perspective, of joy and hope as an antidote to the pain and concern we experience still in this year 2021.

CONTENTS

The Earth Turns

The sky is wide and grey
A veil of silence
Visited by birds
Plunging through its icy depths
Flying soft feathers
Transformed into stars
As night descends
She wraps her veil quietly
Around her sparkling guests

Dark at two
Silence
Too soon awake
And yet the silence
Vibrates
Chill envelopes timelessness
Of incipient morning
As the earth turns

The sky now dark yet blue
Her edges to the east
Uncover golden filaments
Stars hide shyly
Sliding back into a bowl of light
To visit other worlds
While birds awake
And turn the disappearing twinkles
Into song

A Prayer for Peace

We rest in spirit

We rest in prayer

We rest in ideas

We are active and passive

We breathe deeply

We remember those who are a part of us

We think of all who suffer

Of all who dream

Of all who care for others and are endangered

Of all who love

We extend all love beyond our breath

Beyond our peace

Beyond our spirit

Beyond our prayer

We become a garden

Growing from our breath

Growing from our spirit

Within our garden is light

Within that light is peace

Within that peace is a blending of all souls

All souls are a garden of life

All souls become a garden of love

Great spirits guide us through our garden of love

Great spirits lift us

Breathe through us

We become the sigh of all who dream and love and suffer

We become both sigh and laughter

For our garden is both joy and sorrow

We walk outside and inside ourselves

Finding peace within this journey in our garden

All souls are visible and invisible

All souls are beyond gender, race, and labels

All souls breathe with us as one great idea of love

As we breathe together

We feel our connection in a web of love

Our threads connect through a great spirit

Embracing us in peace

Lifting us up to join the world

To be present for the world

To breathe for the world

To touch the world with healing and care

To be stewards and companions of all that is

To seek within the world both justice and harmony

To seek beyond justice a moral compass

Pointing and embracing our souls

Our souls become both life and death in a continuum of love

We are that love

We are that peace

We are each other

An Inconsequential Moon

The moon was full last night
But hidden behind fog, clouds and smoke
She seemed somewhat inconsequential
As a small sphere hiding behind a giant hand
Ruling over the sky like a cosmic god
She might have been a ring on the god's finger
Pure platinum with a cloudy jewel
Testifying to her value
Yet timidly displayed
A mere adjunct
To the hegemony of clouds

There is a Lost City in Colombia

There is a lost city in Colombia
Where people
People called the Tayronas
And the Muisca
Built and dreamed
Built roads and cities
Built roads of stone
Stone houses and dams
Built their cities
From the Pacific to the Atlantic
Loved their families
Loved the land

The land of mountains and Savannas
Of foggy valleys
And snow-capped mountains
Rocked their babies
In the nooks of the Andes
Over land filled with gold
Gold for temple statues
To honor their gods
To honor their ancestors
45,000 years ago
The Caribbean
And the Andean
Highland slopes
Nurtured Pleistocene and Holocene peoples
Living in rocks
Dreaming ideas
Ideas in art and speech
Hunting and planting
Telling stories of the land
Settling in the mountains
And the plains
Cultivating and sharing
Land the Spanish called El Dorado
Land the Spaniards stole
Stole its shining beauty
Stole the plains and gold from their guileless Amerindian hosts
Taking *resguardo*
Land that no one owns
Communal land of the indigenous peoples
Land to share
Land lost to Spanish priests and pillagers
Land lost to all who would
Come and take
Come and take
Come
And take
Muisca the muse
Of the Amerindian
Tells tales of the Bague

The grandmother soul
Who thinks cosmic thoughts of the world
Of the human race
She dances
With Cuza of night
To the sound of a Fo drum
Spirit of music
Bringing space and time
Through air and smoke
To Chibachacum
To Tomsa
Where stars
Land and stone
Brimming in exultation
Spew seeds to light the Milky Way
Placenta of the universe
Turned inside out
Gold marries Chimi
Germinating the seeds
Of all creation
Floods cover the earth
To punish its own creation
Till the falls bring Knowledge
And the rainbow Hope
And the people dream
New dreams
The Spanish pass by
Leaving small pox and Malaria
Their legacy of slavery
Repeating itself in waves
Of exploitation
And pillaging
Of the land
Of the people
Imperial giants
Walk the land
With trucks and tanks
Drills and dynamite
Stealing its coal

Stealing oil and minerals
Enslaving the people
To work the mines
To destroy their own land
To succumb to war
To succumb to exploitation
There is a lost people in Colombia
Seeking their lost stories
A lost people
Half a million refugees
Seeking to return to the land
Of the grandmother soul
Of Bague
Indestructible peoples of Colombia
Dreaming dreams
Dreaming their stories
Of land, mountains, fog and starry skies
Dreaming dreams
Dreaming dreams
Of the grandmother soul
Dreaming cosmic dreams
Of Bague
The grandmother soul
The Creator
Bague
The Grandmother soul

I Am Tiktik Kaanu

I am Tiktik Kaanu
Leaf--cutter anthill in my Rama language
Indigenous land in Nicaragua
I am just a small part of the native land
I hear howler monkeys and the toucan
Calling in my trees
My skirt is green
My arms are vines and trees
Sheltering my people
Who fish in canoes within my veins
Children run in my paths
We harvest fruit and make baskets
As we have done for centuries
But now I worry
Strange people have brought cattle
Strange people have burned my skin
Strange people have killed my people
Cut down my forests
And cut my little children who bleed
And hurt my soul
Sometimes they are murdered as they play in the fields
Their mothers and fathers are murdered too
They do not speak my language
I do not understand why they hurt me and my people
I do not understand why they cut my trees and burn my villages

Some say they need the land for cattle

To kill and sell the meat to other countries

But it is not theirs

Some say they will take it anyway

Because they say my people are worthless

And own nothing

Because they say I am worthless

Because I am green and welcome the rain

Because I sing with the toucan and the parrot

Because I do not want cattle

That will harm my body

Because I know my body is my own

And will never belong to strangers

I am Tiktik Kaanu

I am the land

As my friends and family

Other Kriol villages in Nicaragua

Are the land

And belong to no one

Haiti and Bolivia

Touton Macoude style

Massacres, assassinations

Under Haiti's illegitimate dictator Juvenel Moise

Supported by 12 million US dollars

And a pat on the back by Trump's Pompeo

Reinforces reminders of oppression of the peoples

Of Venezuela, Iran, Cuba, Syria, Lebanon, Palestine

While Bolivia's election is a light in darkness

Reinstates the Morales socialist party

After a turbulent last election

On the heels of attempts to eliminate term limits

Now a new socialist president claims the election

In spite of US millions supporting the opposition

Luis Arce pledges to continue reforms enforcing human rights

And education for all children

A beacon of hope to all nations seeking to throw off their yoke

Of imperialist exploitation

Bolivia hopes for stability

Waiting in Cuba

The sun waits until the day is lit to ascend triumphantly.

To glow in fiery splendor above Cuban skies

To watch Cubans waiting

For buses, for guides, for instructions, for maintenance, for food

They wait in line

Patiently

And yet

Cubans are always ready

To laugh

Cuba is a luxuriously beautiful country washed by the ocean and light rains, clothed in tropical and semi-tropical trees, flowers and ubiquitous plantations of bananas and sugar cane.
Yet, Cuba appears to be a very poor country, its people living often in substandard conditions on infrastructure long in need of renewal.
The Cuban people seem to be a laughing, "don't worry" group---very proud, beautiful, hard-working and brilliant.
The poets are eloquent, as befits the eloquence of Cuba

Chant in quick 4/4 time

Cuba Che Cuba Che Cuba Che Guevara

Bread and orchids for the people

Fight for people's rights

Equity and parity

Never ending, never ending never ending never ending

Revolution

For the people

Cuban Spanish

Listen to Cuban Spanish
Listen to the vowels
Nuances in minor scales
Listen to Cuban speech
Informing all its music
With the beat of history
Palm trees bend in melancholy
Coffee hangs
Coffee drips through hanging sacks
Saturated in water
Boiled in sugar
Cigars made of tobacco leaf
Dried and fermented
In humid heat
Winds continue whispering
Melodies and incantations
Set in Cuban Spanish

Sunset Pillows

Sunset pillows gold and yellow

Make an ocean bed

Darkness falls upon its sweetness

Turning gold to red

Another nighttime pulls its colors

Over Cuban sheets

Havana whispers in the darkness

How soon shall we meet?

Sixty Whispers

Sixty whispers frame the ghostly city

Rising from debris of yesterday

Sixty whispers argue over history

Rubble seawalls dream against the sea

Havana's glorious theater

Reigns sovereign in moonglow

The Prado feeds the Malecon

Beloved seawall promenade

For lovers, fishermen

And youth

Youth who whisper

Sixty whispers

While skinny cats slip silently

Between the shadows

Framed with sixty whispers

Sixty whispers

Serenade

The ghostly city

Of Havana

Havana Morning

Havana's sun wakes darkly
Spilling gold across the sea
Too brilliant for a gentle morning
Glaring bold is she
Mossy rubble smells of algae
Fishers cast their lines
A lonely jogger passes by
Clutching a New York Times
Sea and clouds
Sun and moss
Conspire to lend the day
Reminders of a Cuban night
Spiced salsa, ocean spray

Travels, May 28 to 29 2016

Arrival in Havana

Through Panama City from San Francisco

Hotel Vedado

A walk to the Malecon

The seawall at dawn

The War Memorial

A mother with two children

Dead children

Victims of war

Hang from her arms

My tears are fresh

Travels in the morning

After falling on watered stairs

Cradling bruises and bumps

In the van to Spiritu Sancti

Through dry forests of coconut

And brilliant red blossomed trees

An evening reading of poetry

Coffee on the balcony

Overlooking the city square

A flooded room

From a hardworking cooler system

Spraying rain upon my bed

A blessed city

Spiritu Sancti

Happiness in Cuba

Cuba is iron gates

Sheets of rubble and macadam

People everywhere

Gathering

Waiting

And stray cats

Slipping between puddles

Time stands still

In Cuba

Waiting

With the people

And the cats

Waiting

In line

For instructions

For buses

For news

Don't worry

Everyone laughs

In happiness

In trust

In hope

In Cuba

God Is Lonely

God is lonely
Children are starving
They are still caged at the border
They still drown on their way to freedom
God's family of humanity is estranged
God's family of humanity is lost
Looking for grace
Looking for God
Who gave them sight
Yet they have created
Their own blindness
And cannot comfort God
In loneliness
God looks in love upon the world
As parents observe their children
Wishing them well
And yet sees violence and hate
The children must learn to remedy
Must learn to change
For they themselves are the love
God seeks
In loneliness
Thousands of years ago in Peru
People drew an enormous cat
On the famous Nazca Line

Perhaps hoping God would see it

And be less lonely

They also drew a huge hummingbird

A monkey and a spider

Big enough

For God to see

And laugh

Knowing they could not

Remove God's worries

Could not bring justice to the world

But thought perhaps a large cat

On the hills of Nazca

Might help

Small Play: A New Society

The stage is quiet
Broken bricks and burnt wood lie in the center
A enters with mask in hand
His sign says ENICCAV (VACCINE)
He places it in between two bricks
He sits on a broken wall and waits
B enters
His sign says NOITULOS (SOLUTION)
A: Going somewhere?
B: Maybe
A: May I sit?
B: Six feet away
No, make that ten feet
No mask?
B: Naah.
A: Make that fifteen feet
A puts on a mask
B: Know how long this will last?
A: Who cares? The world's gone as far as I know
Anybody coming by?
B: Dunno
Lady with potatoes enters with mask
Hungry?
A: Yeah, but no money.
Lady: New society, it's all free
Potatoes and oranges
Except for the cigarettes and the beer
They'll cost you
A and B take oranges
Potato lady exits state left
A and B peel oranges
Madame Butterfly enters with mask, in opera costume

A: Where'd you come from?

M. Butterfly: Backstage

I represent the arts

We're free too, but who'll come

Now that everything is destroyed

Sings, "Un bel di........"

Tough to sing with a mask....*Exits*

A—weird world

B---I'll say.

A: I just figured out the new normal

B: Yeah?

A: All this free stuff.

We find lots of it, hoard it

And sell it

You know, black market

The poor get rich

Instead of the rich people

Isn't that the way it's supposed to be?

Now that the world we knew is burnt down

And there's no property

The poor get to get rich

And change society

B: yeah. What's the change?

Wonder if a bus will come

It'd be great if they took me to Eniccav (Vaccine)!

And you'd go to Noitulos (Solution)

We'd have a vaccine and a solution, Woohoo!

A: Yeah, and we'll get rich. Selling free stuff.

Man enters with two sticks

These are self-driving sticks. They're free.

Each takes one

A and B:-Thanks

Man- Good luck.

All exit stage

Pig

Why do we use brutal words

Pig

Swine

To name such pink beauty

Wallowing in grace

Among amazing mud slurries

Brilliant pigs

Whose minds can fathom mysteries

Which delicate hooves

Cannot describe in pen and ink

Why do we use such brutal words

Pig

Swine

To name subtle intelligence

Far more astute than that of swan

Or hummingbird

With graceful names yet smaller brains

A snorting snout that burrows and buries

Deep in sloppy humus stew

Yet once I saw a small child

Kiss a pig's wet snout

Affection and affinity

Of species pig and child

Nameless in knowledge

They should be friends

Awaiting Grace

Breathing in rain

Inhaling life pristine pockets emptying from rosy dark sky

Damp blinding drops of pulsing moisture

Penetrating every naked pore

Face and hands

Welcoming rain

Welcoming clean memories to be made

Across the Arabian Sea

Red Sea, Gulf of Aden Persian Gulf

Await cleansing

That will not come

Four dozen men less one

Are executed on a dry warm day

Absent rain absent blessing

In the land of Mecca

Land of holy pilgrimage

Flowers of holiness

Cut from vibrant stems

To drip red salt

Upon a yielding earth

Opening her arms

To catch those drops

Of grace

Stretching further still

To cast her shadow

On the poet's cell

Fahradh, I am your mother too

I wait beneath the prison

That cannot claim your voice

I wait and watch here where

No pristine rain may fall

No cleansing fount may purify those

Who cut the radiant blossoms

From their stems

I wait

My pores exhale the rosy sky

Across the sea from other worlds

My arms reach out to raise your soul

Into a pristine night

And all I breathe is poetry

And pulsing drops

Of blinding light

On January 2, 2016, Sheikh Nimr al Nimr, a man of peace who led anti-government protests, and 46 others, mostly Saudi, were executed simultaneously in twelve cities and four prisons, some by beheading, some by firing squad; most were Sunni Muslims accused of terrorism; Sheikh al Nimr was considered a leader among the Shiite minority. Shortly before this act, the Palestinian Ashraf Fahradh was condemned to death—his sentence has since been appealed and is now 800 lashes, 8 years in prison, and public repentance for his criticism of the Saudi government

The Sidewalk

The sidewalk caught me again!
Laughed a young girl
Awkward embarrassed
As she slipped on the concrete
Managing not to fall
The sidewalk caught me again!
The sidewalk
Cracked face
Quake-ravaged tiles
Indolently lies in wait
For those of us
Hurrying from corner to corner
Who become easily trapped
Into stepping on a crack!
Never break your mother's back
While the slogans
Caught within
Tiles of concrete
Become memories
Of scraped knees
And childhood
Games in chalk
Hopscotch and rocks
The sidewalk caught me again!

Chairs

Chairs seem almost human

Four legs, a back, sometimes arms

Often scars and scratches

All too human

In the fragile face

They offer the world

Too human

In their vulnerability

Even the word

Chair

Sounds vulnerable

Timid

Lost without a table

Or perhaps another chair

Lost in the middle of a room

Waiting

For its fragile

Human equivalent

To sit

I Wake Early

I wake early

The night still deep

The early skateboarder on the street

Before the cars take possession

A flicker on the horizon

Not a star

A reflected light

From someone else's window

A streetlight glares below

Garbage trucks begin their routine

Listening to the sounds

I escape my own thoughts

Of what I could have done

Better

Many years ago

Genocide is in the news

Genocide is in the news again
As if there were no possible respite from rape
Respite from murder
Ethnic cleansing with blood
One million children killed in the Shoah
Two million women
Three million men
A holocaust not by fire
But intentional
Heartless purging of innocence
Inflicted by our own species
Guatemala in 1982
Babies thrown down a well
Two boys survive
Try to hide from the memory
Until a phone call wakes them to the
Nightmare of their childhood
Now in Pakistan and Afghanistan
Genocide of the Hazara
Reminds us of other genocides
Semitic, Persian, Armenian, African, Native American, Asian
Indigenous peoples across the globe
Worshipping the wrong god at the wrong altar
Or on a desirable piece of land
On oil perhaps
Or diamonds
Or gold

Or simply in the wrong place

At the wrong time

Convenient victims

Of someone else's power hungry talons

The Hazara

Half of them driven from their homeland

A child bears a sign on her cheeks

"Kill" "Shia"

Shia refuse to be ruled by Sunni

And are exterminated

Taliban kill 3,000 of their Hazara prisoners in 1997

They murder 8,000 more in 1998

The village of Mazar-i-sharif

Holds the dead on its streets

Unburied against religious law

Until the Taliban allow burial

Due to the stench

For reasons of hygiene

They are finally buried

The murders continue

In the year 2000

Ismaili Hazara moving between settlements

On the Robatak Pass

Are detained four months

Before being executed

A year later in Bamyan Province, Afghanistan

Three hundred Hazara are taken hostage

170 men are first killed

Including humanitarian workers

Women and children observe
Until their turn comes
Sunni, Taliban, military
Repudiate and murder Hazara
In Karachi
In Quetta
Eight hundred dead
Fifteen hundred wounded
In 2011 Hazara Town massacre
and Mastung Bus Shooting
Leave over thirty dead
In 2012 Hazaras are killed in Quetta
And fleeing Pakistan
Lashkar-e-Jhangvi vows to kill Shia
Hazara-Shia
To make Pakistan clean
Pakistan
Land of the pure
Must rid the world of the unclean
People descended from
Genghis Khan
Persian, Pakistani, Afghan, Mughal
Sharing the Hazara diaspora
Sharing the Shia legacy
Are not Sunni
Are not clean
Are not worthy to live
The boat of Hazara people
Bound from Indonesia to Australia

To seek asylum
The year, 2012
Sinks
Other boats pass by
And do nothing
To help the unclean
At last plucked from the sea
The Hazara choose to starve
Rather than return to their enemies
On January 10, 2013
One hundred thirty Hazara
Are killed in Quetta
Two hundred seventy are wounded
By bombs targeting Hazara-Shia
Five days ago
Just five days ago
More Hazara die
The year is young
The year is young
Time enough for
Ethnic cleansing
Of the unclean
Children down a well
Civilian assassinations
Black against white against black
Or brown or grey or yellow
How many more
Bodies must be destroyed
To make the world clean?

Murder of Palestinians

According to Haaretz Israeli news

November 25, 2012

Since the first Qassam rocket

Fell on Israel in April 2001

59 Israelis have been killed

4,717 Palestinians and counting

Have been eliminated with Israeli bombs

Mostly civilians and children

Golda Meir said

There is no such thing as a Palestinian

If you don't exist

Can you be murdered?

In March, 2001, Mandela wrote to Thomas Friedman: "Apartheid is a crime against humanity. Israel has deprived millions of Palestinians of their liberty and property. It has perpetuated a system of gross racial discrimination and inequality. It has systematically incarcerated and tortured thousands of Palestinians, contrary to the rules of international law. It has, in particular, waged a war against a civilian population, in particular children." (Nelson Mandela)

The Moon Behind Night Clouds

The moon gazes coolly

From behind her round veil

Prepared to jump through transparent cloth

And rip its fragile luminescence

Tearing the hymen of the sky

A poet is jailed for life (Jasmine)

A poet is jailed for life

A poet

For speaking his poem

Jasmine

Jasmine, the flower of the country, Tunisia

The flower of the Arab Spring

Tunisians call their revolution Dignity, not Jasmine

Inspired by the self-immolation of a street merchant

The Dignity Revolution

The newspapers call it

Jasmine in honor of a poet

Muhammed ibn al-Dheeb al-Ajami

Jailed in November 2012

Evokes the pride of the Tunisian flower

Beautiful and ubiquitous in its perfume

Jasmine

To praise the revolution of the people

Whose refusal to accept corruption

Unemployment

Humiliation

Leads to a new order

And the words of a poet in Qatar

Asking that the demands of freedom

Be met by his own Sheik

His own government

Whose Article 53 of a repressive Constitution

Protects an oppressive regime

Makes criticism illegal

And condemns a poet

Absent from his own trial

To life imprisonment

And yet one cannot muzzle a poet

Any more than one can muzzle the perfume

Of the ubiquitous Jasmine

Muhammed ibn al-Dheeb al-Ajami was jailed in November 2012
His "Jasmine Poem" was critical of his government. He was arrested
over words critical of Sheikh Hamad bin Khalifa al-Thani

Three Nights the Moon

For three nights the moon hung like a cradle

Seeming neither to wax nor wane

Resting serenely,

Rocking quietly above its earthen parent

Suspended in space and time

Orbiting at uncanny speeds

And yet still unmoved

Indifferent

While pulling tides

And issuing forth

Magnetic

Moon dust

Rural Homeless (Observations on the Tuareg, called "rebels" fighting Mali Army, January, 2013)

Rural homeless

Are like urban homeless

Nomads on earth

Victims of boundaries

Once free to roam and live

Within the natural cycles of drought and rain

Now caught by barbed wire

Or roving military agents of property owners

And their foreign colonial agents

Telling them to move on

Move on

Or come back and we will give you money

Money and food

For your dignity and your homes and your land

But even the money is a mirage

Like all promises of the colonialists

Tuareg nomads

Nomads from the Sahel

Tell stories of living sand dunes

Who create the giraffe from sun and sand

They wear blue veils against the yearly Harrmattan winds

Ride the giraffe and the camel

And fight for their freedom

But the sand dunes

And the giraffe
Can no longer
Define their life
Or sustain their body
And their ancient soul
Reflected still in dance
And the Berber language
Of Tamasheq
Encroaching property lines
Are mutilating the body
Of the Tuareg
How shall they heal?
And with them
The desert?

Out of the Dust Comes Life

Out of the dust comes life
Out of the dust comes the mother spirit
The spirit of the desert
Her voice can be heard in the hyena, the wolf
The birds of the desert
And the creatures that make the desert home
Her footsteps can be felt in the moving dunes
The rustling of her garments in the winds of Harrmattan
Blowing inexorably throughout the dry season
Dehydrating and breaking trunks of trees
As the spirit of the desert moves south on the Sahara
To the Gulf of Guinea
Blinding even the mighty sun
With crowds of living, blowing dust particles
Ishumar Tuareg move through Niger, Algeria, Libya, Mali
Paperless or multiple-papered and carded
With plural citizenships meaning nothing
Moving with the spirit mother to the symphony of desert sounds
Sounds in the silence
Sounds of alone
Sounds of the mountain
Sounds of colors
Sounds of age
Of paintings now 14,000 years old
Ishumar Tuareg celebrate their spirit mother

Celebrate their revolution of mind and sound

Vision and spirit

Their revolution of quiet and alone

Their revolution of the mother spirit

The spirit of the desert

The Sunset

I am told the desert sunset is extraordinary

In its pink and red, blue, yellow and orange tones

I have seen glorious sunsets everywhere

In Florence, flung across the whole sky

Above Renaissance domes and dwellings

In Africa, as the sun descended, an enormous globe,

encompassing half the horizon of Zimbabwe

In Germany, rising in layers upward in purples, greens, oranges

and lavenders

In France, pristinely beautiful above the Loire

In San Francisco, now pale violet and pink hovering above dusk

And freshly lighted windows

Reflecting back the sun and silent secrets

Sunsets clamor against the imagination

Demand undisturbed audience

Demand acknowledgement

Of a miracle

A pause in disbelief

Volcanoes of the Sahara

Create a sinuous body

She lies under the melting sun

Turns her back on the shining moon

Naked against the horizon

She sleeps on the Sahara

Hot breasts point upward

Rising from the desert

Mother Emi Koussi and sisters

Still vibrating and churning

Underneath the desert

Exhausted and yet waiting

For their earth lover

To awaken them again

To hot erotic fecundity

Stretch lazily

Distanced from the

Enormous, undulating crater

Forty kilometers long in Mauritania

Folding back on the earth

Five hundred million years

Offering its immense navel

To an indifferent sky

We Walk

We walk a path of questions
A path unknown
A path of new impressions
We walk alone
We walk a path of tension
Envisioning each step
Incipient imaginings
Contrive to intercept
Ideas in hidden shadows
Ideas under dark stones
Ideas waiting for answers
To their own sparkling tones
Conceived in random images
Conceived in random thought
In footfalls just above them
Sounds and dreams not yet sought
From eyes gazing through leaning trees
Ears listening for naught
But whispers in a scented breeze
Mind waiting to be taught

Retirement Home Visit

How can I eat? She asks me

I am hungry

I show her where the dining room is

She has forgotten again

Each day she forgets

Where am I? Another asks

She shows me her hands

Lined with white flecks

I have lost my papers

She says

I take her

Gently

To an assistant

She dreams of

Lost papers

Now I am in the piano room

A lady comes in early

She says

I always wanted to play the piano

I am cheated if you play

Instead of me

I want to play

She looks down at her hands

Sadly

But I never learned how

Evening Benediction

The hand of twilight

Sprays magic from its fist

Opening suddenly in golden softness

Throwing jewels upon the sky

Spilling red wine among the clouds

Streaming through the sky

In Bacchanalian bliss

The Greater Scheme of Things

The greater scheme of things

Find in a rainbow or a sunset

Drink from a star or a drop of water

Fold up in polyphonic illuminations

Emanating everywhere

In each drop we sing

Each cadence resolved

Or unresolved

Reflected back

Through stardust

*The greater scheme of things is in a rainbow or a sunset or a
star or a drop of water. It doesn't matter. We are everywhere;
it's a question of perspective; we are neither safe nor protected
nor lost; we simply are, and that's enough to know that touch
can sing and worries are only fantasy.*

Touch and Silence

Touch is ephemeral

Aromas evaporate into ether

Esters of dreams

Hide under quilts

Sewn by Puck's crew

Dancing in a mid-summer night

On the wings of hummingbirds

Dipping through their dreams' reflections

Etched with dew

Through mushroom gills

Emanating vapors

Dreamlike cobwebs

Sliding through each needle's eye

To find the way to fly

To find the why of sky

Through meadows' patterns

Cats' paws

Wagging tails

Waltzing through earth tones

Into sienna sounds

Of silence

The comet got lost

The comet we waited for got lost

Or burned up close to the sun

Or perhaps just melted away

Like the wicked witch in a pail of water

Snow and ash, ice and sand

Dashing through the universe

Just another shooting star

Another Hale Bop inspiring suicides

Lost in death

Lost in space

Bodies offering their spirits

To tails of comets

Aspiring to ride bodies of ice

Shooting bodies spinning through space

Like those comets who crashed into earth eons ago

To give us water

To give us life

Comets melt into planets

And create life

Or fly like Icarus

Too close to a sun or star

And disappear

Leaving only

Clicking red shoes

One

One
Immutable
One existence
Or non-existence
One world
And all beyond
One interdependence
Of galaxies
Dark matter
Light
Unfathomable cold
Explosive heat
One aspen forest
Of interconnection
Beneath the soil
All matter
And anti-matter
Connecting in
Vibrating energy
One laughter
One snowflake
Individual
Irreplaceable
Tiny
Oneness
Unique
Single
Made whole
In solo smiles
Generating
One
Universal joy

Life is Free (song)

I thought that I'd waited for someone like you
For someone with strength in his heart
But I've been there before
When a heart was still sore
And I know it could keep us apart
I'll blow you a kiss for the wind to bring home
I'll send you a smile in the breeze
I'll wish you the wishes that hope can design
But I won't ever wait for a love that's not mine
No, I don't want a love that's not mine

Life is Free
And life is a fantasy
Golden dreams in a bowl
Woven in cobwebs
Of silk and of stars
Silver beams shine through my soul
Catch me a star
And I'll find you a galaxy
Hide me in oceans of foam
Don't wake me up
Till you've answered the mystery
Don't wake me up till I'm home
Don't wake me up
Till I'm home

Death Walks

Thanatos walks darkly

Thanatos walks

Her journey covers shadows and blood

Her journey is everywhere

In fields of war and devastation

In cradles, beds, meadows and rivers

Cities and villages

Thanatos

A muse herself

A muse of death

Seeking transformation

Seeking redemption

Seeking life

Thanatos

Behind the mirror weeping

Thanatos

Hiding in the tomb

Reaching for light

Thanatos seeks her lover Eros

To transform death

To transform war

To transform destruction

To transform darkness

To lose herself

In love

Texts for tiles in a public place

Minnesota Woman

She came across the Bering Bridge

8,000 years ago

Alone she died and left no child

Upon her neck was hung a fragile shell

And on her waist an elk horn dagger

Freedom

Dred Scott fought

For the right to be free

Rights not espoused

In our original Constitution

The flame he lit

Sparked our Civil War

And still burns today

Wakan Tanka

Wakan

Spirit world

Bring peace to all

Wakan Tanka

Divine mystery

Hold us all in love

BOUQUET

Violet

Violence
Violate
Violet, the gentle flower
Born and clothed
To be victim
Not perpetrator
Of violence
Yet facing upward
Bravely
Like a purple lion
Gentle face
Framed with petals
A lion's mane
Gazing at the world
With noble trust
Purple lion
Pansy viola
Purple violet
So like violence
Or violate
In the choice and sequence of letters
So close are violence and victim
Violence and violet
Violence occurs at home
In gardens
Where violets grow
To smile upon the world
In purple bliss
So unaware of boots
And scissors
Expecting nothing
But wind and rain
And sunshine
Expecting love
Inviolate love for violets

Lei Flowers

Tuberose, pikake, ginger, plumeria
Float above the Hulu
Brush and breathe
Fragrant seductions
Whisper quietly
Talking story
Summoning the tales
Of whales and
Humuhumunukunukuapua'a
Swimming gracefully
In warm and tranquil waters
Telling of the wind
Singing of the moon
Chanting of the days gone by
Rustling on soft golden shoulders
Perfumed petals
Waiting to be lifted
And thrown upon the salty waves
To speak forever memories

Dandelion

Not a dandy lion
Primping his yellow hair
But a lion's tooth
Löwenzahn
A dental lion
Sweeping through the garden
The lion's teeth demanding imperial passage
Till every worm route beneath the garden
Is guarded by dandelions
Their roots twining and intertwining
In a perpetual war for the garden above
Tooth stems pushing upwards
Imbedding themselves in green mouths
Shoving green buds upward
Becoming green saw teeth
And skinny yellow petals
Children love to rub beneath their chins
Turning soft skins yellow
And when the wind turns cool
Becoming parachutes of cotton silk
Floating, catching everywhere
Cotton teeth like cotton candy
Sticky, sticking, ubiquitously
Flicking all their seedy eloquence
Biting with soft teeth
Into new fecund ground
To plunge again
Their tongues into the garden
And rise again as lion's teeth
As lion's teeth
Dent de lion
Dandelion

Orchid

Pandora's Lulu
Sings of the orchid
Smell me
At night
When my fragrance overwhelms
Cloaking in seductive scents
Soft twining beauty
Thrusting roots
Around each
Ready waist or chest or leg
Hanging in fierce tenderness
To catch moist lips
Of humid winds
And sweet perspiring
Clitoral embraces
Singing sticky sensuality
Wrapped in velvet music

Baby's Breath

Gypsophila paniculata
Panicles of tiny flowers
Spray above the garden rocks
Timid baby fingers
Explore their space
To explode in white torrents
Soft miniatures
Of flowers
Born to adorn a rock
Stolen to accompany
A lover's bright bouquet of wildflowers
Of wildflowers and
Baby's sweet whispered breath

Rose

A rose rests upon the covered table
In a small retort
Gazing out the window
Its petals curling back
Frayed and brown
It has no fragrance
Its frail life spent
Upon a restaurant table
Perfume exhausted
Colors dulled
Remembering
A garden time
A blooming
Remembering
A time of shiny red
Rose petals
Sunshine
And sweet smells
Remembering a rose

Daisy

Flower of the meadows
Marguerite, innocently
Plucking petals
He loves me, loves me not
Loves me
Daisy
White bridal gown
With golden head
Long stemmed legs
Pushing happily
Into green fields
Topped with smiling daisies
Gathered into a bouquet
Of many or a few
Picked by children
Or strolling lovers
Offered as a modest
Gift of spring joy
Daisies strung together
As a wreath
To adorn a child's tousled locks
Or a bride's hair
Smugly ensconced in a lapel
Tucked behind an ear
A name
Marguerite
Daisy
Born to love and smile
And be seduced
In innocence
To find sorrow or joy
In guileless daisyness

Magnolia

Ancient, headily perfumed
Magnolia
145 to 65 million years old
Pre-Cretaceous magnolia
Opening gloriously
Into the world
 Pollinated by beetles
Tough and resilient flowers
Accommodating loving intrusions
Of tank like bugs
Padding firmly on bracts
Not soft petals
Intruding on sturdy Inflorescence
Witnessing millennia
Witnessing ages of life
Offering deep perfumes
To dinosaurs
Surviving their rapacious
Mouths
And claws
Surviving floods
Fires
Hurricanes and cyclones
Surviving
Yet now in danger of extinction
By the human species
Clearing forests
Killing the magnolia
For
Bananas
And coffee

Cherry blossom

Sakura
From Okinawa to Kyoto and Tokyo
Ephemeral blossoms
Clouds of pink beauty
Spreading petals
Inviting hanami
Peaceful gatherings
Picnics
Gifts from Japan
To Washington DC
And Vancouver
Gifts of peace
And beauty
Blowing exquisite pink petals
Around a world
Seeking peace

Lupine

Our cat
Hidden in a field of lupine
Lifts her head
Delicious golden softness
Outlined on purple
Her whiskers are flecked with
Silver grey hairs
From soft green leaves
Tied under
Saucy blue bonnets

Tulip

Tulips began their journey somewhere
Along a corridor from Northern China
To Southern Europe
Persians extolled their beauty
Their center of diversity
The Hindu Kush, Pamir
The Tien Shan Mountains
Between central Afghanistan
And northern Pakistan
Tulip gardens formed
A carpet for warriors to rest
And hold counsel
Gathering shy perennials
Into mountain caves
Admiring their bright cups
Setting to one side
These glorious
Ambassadors of peace
And beauty
Witnesses of plans of men
To conquer or acquire
Nature's land and treasures
Or religious domination
Blind to the perfect plan of peace
Flowering beside them
Tulips were beloved of the Ottomans
And found their way to Holland
When the poet Clusius praised them
His garden was robbed
Of the now precious flowers
Precious because the great poet praised hem
And Holland was set ablaze with tulips

Iris

Fleur-de-lis, golden iris
Sprung from the House of Capet
Coat of Arms of Florence and Ukraine
Flag of Brussels
Lost love of Calderon's Broken Vows
Weeping, bearded iris
Frantic, dancing irises of Van Gogh
Purple, imperious
Yet multi-colored
Greek goddess of the rainbow
Messenger of sky and sea
Messenger of sorrow

Gladiola

Gladiolas from sub Saharan Africa
Claim to be irises
But they arise from corms
Not bulbs
More like crocuses
Gladiolas find themselves
In strange surprise
Next to a garden wall
Or path
Thrusting upwards
As sword lilies
Guarding the garden path

Daffodil

The restaurant on the corner
Set out tables with a daffodil
On each table
Bright spots of light
At seven in the morning
A chilly spring morning
The tables were bare of guests
For breakfast
Yet inspiration
For passers by
Seeing
Daffodils of light
Bright yellow warmth
Standing tall
Against the cold

Ficus

The Ficus wraps its smooth, tawny arms
Around a long dead parent
Supporting that stump of past glory
There on the corner
The Ficus holds in strange embrace
A trunk of decaying fabric
Pressing vibrant limbs around its bulk
In a slow urban dance

Poppy

Poppies are not poppies
They say
Poppies
California poppies
Are not poppies at all
Afghanistan poppies
Are war booty
Or excuses for war
Against drugs
Poppies explode
Across the meadows
In Monet's painting
Of poppies
Gently making way
For a lady with a bonnet
And a little boy
Admiring
Poppies

Fennel

The fennel flower
Nigella sativa
Delicate
Aromatic
Scents of licorice
And grain
A cure for
Common ailments and allergies
A known healer
For ages upon ages
For birds and animals
Including human creatures
Now Nestlé would own the rights
To fennel
Would patent fennel
Would claim its cures
As property rights
So birds and animals
Including human creatures
Would need to litigate
To enjoy
Just possibly
The restorative
And soothing
Loveliness and balm
Of the Fennel
Would need the
Services of lawyers
To cut through laws
Of privatization
To seek a natural cure
From the sweet
Fennel flower
Growing from
Our own
Mother
Earth

Epic a Rose

Epic a rose
Lyric its aroma
Dramatic its grace
Carpets of petals
Softly sensual
Evoke
Tastes of rose hip
Singing splashes
Colors of sunsets
Songs of birds
Soft stories
Told by the wind
Offering bouquets
Of beauty
Twined with memory

Within a Flower

Within a flower
Velvet intricacies
Folded petals
Open to delicate stamen
Welcoming bees
And hummingbirds
Into a dance pf destiny
Shedding pollens
Breathing perfumes
Inspiring bouquets
Wreaths
Garlands
Leis
And sneezes

Dahlia

Infinite variety in petals and colors
Beloved of the Aztec
Seduced Spaniards
Who took her back to Spain
From Mexico
And then to Holland
Where she nearly perished
On board a ship
But for one tuber
That survived and flourished
With pointed petals
In a bright pink ring
Dense with color
And soft grace

De Young Annual Flower Show

Flower arrangements fill the art gallery

Displayed before paintings

Less graphic than their flower commentary

Tracks of grass

Fire in Los Angeles

Broken fence wire, dark ripped rags

Brilliant flowers attempting regeneration

Rising in another corner from metallic waste

A little boy places flowers carefully in chicken wire

While his mother busies herself with the bouquet

Praising her small son as I pass

Ferrets are all Business
(a tribe of ferrets is called a "business")

Ferrets are all business

Closely caucusing each day

Sliding, squirreling, slipping

Into deep discussion of

Numerical analyses of

Mercurial mercantile schemes

Tribal ferreting meriting

Descriptions of their day

Simply what you would expect

From ferrets

Business as usual

Light Emitting Diode Towers of Villarreal on Bay Bridge

Sunday's moon in San Francisco

Waning crescent of bent sliver

Hides aloft in silent envy

Far above the lighted towers of Villarreal

Towers of light

Independent sparkling moments

Sequenced separately

Find design

Like chords of music

Floating flocking

Climbing upwards

Swimming diving

Jumping over radiant ferries

Chugging through the shining

Waters of the bay

Underneath a sequined bridge

Where above wheeled motors ride

Following their destinations

Shadowed clouds disintegrate

In shattered animated jewels

Spinning brightly in white light

Dancing past the hiding crescent

Of the moon

On Sunday night

International Ocean Film Festival, Pier 39

From the screen plunge sharks and enormous waves

Images of water play upon the walls of the theater

Flowing into the energy of body surfers

Daring or acquiescing to the ocean's moving walls

Curling and crashing on the shore

People move among the chairs, shuffling quietly

Pausing

Or congregate in groups, emptying through the doors

Chattering

Land creatures, bound to gravity and air

Unable to emulate those graceful compatriots of the ocean

Heavy, ponderous, encumbered

Habitants of land

Dwelling on this side of the mirror

Observing whales gamboling serenely

Through a marine window

Chairs observe the mirror in grey blueness

Observe a royal purple curtain

And a shiny stage

Shining like the back of a wet dark whale

Stage right a simple table stands

Where boxes march solemnly

Waiting to confer themselves

Upon the divers and filmmakers

Who have captured the other side of the mirror

Pollution Blows North

The Inuit
Close to nature
Close to the heart of mother earth
Enduring millennia upon millennia
Of nature's harsh lessons of tough love
Born of conditions the earth has created
Simply existing
Evolving
Revolving
And spinning through seasons
Balanced upon a revolving globe
As part of its pattern
Essential to its character
Non-essential to its existence
Drinking once fresh
Unadulterated waters
Consuming fresh game and fish and plants
Breathing untainted air
From healthy lungs of earth
Enjoying unsullied paradise
On a singing planet
Taught and raised in a challenging
Garden of Beginnings
Finding nourishment from rich clean soils
From pristine streams and oceans

Finding refuge in caves

Or sheltering under detritus of reeds and trees

Building families communities societies

To live with the earth in harmony

In the arctic hemisphere

In harmony with the earth

Pollution blows north

Pollution from non-Inuit peoples

Who exploit the earth

Who will not learn to sing and dance

With earth as partner

Who will not learn

To breathe the lungs of earth

Sweet vibrant membranes

With pure untainted breath

Pollution blows north

Pollution blows north to the Inuit

Blows north from China

Blows north from the Americas

Blows north with toxins

Blows north to poison

Once-thriving fishing villages

Blows north to suffocate the living tundra

Blows north with asthma and cancer

Blows north to rock the Inuit with winds of death

Against its cradle

Write-Offs for the IRS

Someone I love told me

Heartache, stress and loneliness

Should be write-offs for the IRS

More debilitating than debt

Or perhaps more defining of debt

Than debt itself

Being in the hole

A metaphor for loss

Isolation

Impenetrable boundaries

Being in the red

Falling through space

In a manhole

Painted with the blood

Of a manacled monster

Undefinable

Yet present

In the mirror

Staring, cuffed, tethered

Watching you

Reach out

To shatter the mirror

Nelson Mandela Dies (December 5, 2013)
In Memoriam

Nelson Mandela
Madiba
As a child lovingly named Rolihlahla,
"Troublemaker"
Was called Nelson when he went to school
Became father of modern Africa
Son of ancient Africa
A light to all
Passing in the dark
Has faded into the last horizon
Yet glows still
Bearing testimony to peace
Bearing testimony to justice
Child of the veld
Child of Qunu
Shepherd to goatherds
Herds that taught him
A leader waits behind
Inspiring others to find their way
Nelson Mandela
Waited behind 27 long years
Imprisoned on Robbin Island
Waited for justice
Waited across the sea from Qunu
Where memories became reality
Until his freedom graced the whole of Africa
Graced the whole of earth
Graced the whole of humankind
Madiba
Light of Africa
Light of peace
We mourn your passing

Light and Shadow Play

Light and shadow play across the land
Small land parcel
Patio
Large red umbrella sliced by mottled posts
Shading no one
Nothing
Undergarment grey in shadows
Free of stains
Scars upon a naked red top
Facing the sun boldly
Across a dancing garden
Sunk in shade
Hypotenuse draws itself
Against a green house
Dividing light from shadow
A bare tree stands undressed
Before a flowering lilac
Sparkling with tones purple violet green
Sunshine shades each particle
Reflects
Benches invite visitors
To sit above the land
Shading in layers
Under flowered trees
Flowered skirts
Anonymous
Amorous
Land
A backdrop wall
Upstage
Makes mottled
Shadow play

Poetry of Poverty in San Francisco

Poverty lives abundantly in San Francisco
10,000 homeless call its streets home
1 in 4 children and 1 in 5 adults
Go to bed hungry
Malnourished
Somewhere in San Francisco
Nearly 16,000 families face hunger daily
A city of immense wealth
Shuffles over malnourished children
While on the other side of the world
Seven hundred years ago
In medieval Europe
Children and the poor
Filled the prisons
Because they could not pay taxes
In San Francisco
In the year 2013
Children and the poor
Fill the streets
Because they cannot
Find homes
The world's wealthiest 100 people
Earned 240 billion dollars last year
Their wealth could end poverty
Four times over
No one owns our water, air and land
It is held in trust for all
The gap between rich and poor
Accelerates through miasmatic fog
Poverty lives abundantly in San Francisco

Memories Connect (published in Street Sheet, January 2014)

Memories

Connecting with memories

Link with past, present, future

Transmission of thoughts

Images

Interpretations

Impressions

Everything is contingent

Everything is related

The collective forgets

What it wills not to remember

The subconscious remembers

Visiting trauma upon memories

Forgotten

Yet extant like corms

Within the collective consciousness

Tautology

Repeats truth

Breaking out of the same egg

Again and again

Refusing not to be born

Can you stop the train

Speeding from never

To never?

Gardens and War

Kashmir is the most militarized zone in the world

Kashmir has the largest tulip garden in Asia

Try to reconcile gardens with war

The world is meant to be a garden

Where all may share the beauty

And the fruits of the earth

Iraq was once the Garden of Eden

At the convergence of the Tigris and Euphrates

Where agriculture began

And the wheel discovered

Marshes of the indigenous Ma'dan

Marshes drained and destroyed by Saddam

Now find their way back to bulrushes

Fit to hide a baby Moses

As the river is again set free

Babylon awakes and dreams

Of Nebuchadnezzar building his Hanging Gardens

Babylonian gardens for a queen or concubine

Who longed for the mountains of Media

Or perhaps by a Syrian monarch for a lover

Who longed for the gardens of Persia

Iraq and iran

Like Kashmir

Like Lebanon

Lands of gardens

Lands of war

Where Gilgamesh

Traveled to the Garden of the Gods

To Palestine's Mount Hermon

Sumerian gardens

Where gods played

Where centuries before Noah was born

An arc was built to save the animals from a flood

And later still god and man protected the land

From freezing temperatures

So the gardens would sing again

In the sunshine

Gardens of the Golan Heights

Gardens of Syria and Palestine

Yearning for their past

Free from war

Yearning for

Indigenous gardens

Where all people may be free

Where water may flow freely

Among all peoples

And fruits and beauty

Be enjoyed by all

Equally

In gardens

Of peace

The Other

The other
The nameless
My shadow
The other side of the mirror
The other side of earth
The light at the end of a ditch
Dug from here to there
The other
The one in prison
The one who is tortured for telling truth
Refusing to lie
Literally physically
Metaphorically
Refusing to sacrifice integrity
The other
Reflecting back to the sun
Colors and languages
Different myriad varied
Reflecting to the moon
Images of the spirit
Emanating from stripped bones
Or translucent skin
Emanating from ideas
Arising from earth's waters
Incorruptible though polluted

Like sin introduced from outside

Unacceptable

Unwelcome

Untranslatable

Oil on water

Separated into distinct entities

Divided corruption

Divided poisons

Becoming distinct vapors

Becoming new gifts

Diseases and ugliness

Transformed into beauty

Transformed into

The other

Disappearing from the tomb

To appear pristine

Cleansed by absorption into

The other

Singing of millennia past

Languages unknown yet known

By other moments

Other spirits

Reaching through a miasma

Transformed into angelic mist

Of collective

Other

Columbus Street, San Francisco

I walk down Columbus Street
In North beach, San Francisco
Observing the same jacket
Modeled on its stand
Stitches riding across the lapel
A Chinese tailor's shop
Dating back to 1948
When Israel evicted the Palestinians
From 5,000 square miles of Palestine
Taken away from them
By the United Nations
Not that there is a stitch of relevance
To that observation
And yet time stands still
At the tailor's shop
Just as next door
Or two doors down
The shop with famous coffee
Shows the same display I saw in 1995
Perhaps it was the same
In 1948
When I was five years old
I will be seventy this year
And Palestine has lost
Its land
Its people are besieged
And exploited
By Israel's giant friend
The United States
The tailor's shop
Still stands on Columbus
Coffee is produced

Two doors down
Merely a drop
In the global
History
Of exploitation
Giants spar off
Across the world
At the expense
Of their peoples
Factories burn
Or implode
In Bangladesh
Or any other poor country
Scrambling to serve
The imperialist dollar
By exploiting those
With no power
Powerful nations
Hold their own citizens
Or immigrants hostage
To crumbs of pennies
Not sufficient to bake a loaf of treasure
Sufficient to feed their families
Is there no end to injustice?
Wealth breeds more wealth
Devouring the larvae of poverty
To nurture itself
And yet the butterfly
Remains free

Non Violence

Non-violence brings fewer casualties than violence
They
The amorphous they
Want to prove this with statistics
Bombs dropped by remote controlled drones
Bring fewer casualties
To American soldiers
Than bombs dropped by live non remote soldiers
Civilians
Children who are not Americans
Die daily
Are in terror
Daily
They are non-violent
They watch the sky daily
For drones
Non-violence brings fewer casualties than violence
Those are not my words
They are a quotation from somewhere
Children without weapons die in schools
Shot by children with weapons
Who have been abused
By violence
The violence of neglect
The violence of silence
The violence of betrayal
The violence of watching children
Somewhere else
Watch drones threatening
Violence
From azure blue
Peaceful skies

San Francisco
Invests in Fossil Fuels

San Francisco

City of *Recology*

City of Eco-justice

Aiming for no waste

For carcinogen-free air

Proud of bicycles

Emission free buses

San Francisco

City of organic gardens

Gardens at city hall

San Francisco

Asking for higher standards

Than the rest of the nation

For less polluted streets

Less polluting cars

San Francisco

Priding itself on

Sensitivity to climate change

Priding itself on

Sensitivity to social and environmental justice

Smoke-free restaurants and safe streets

San Francisco

Investing

One-half billion dollars

In carcinogenic fossil fuels

One-half billion dollars

In cancer

One-half billion dollars

In hypocrisy

Half a billion dollars

And another million

In firearms and ammunition

San Francisco

City of Saint Francis

City of hope

Our nation and our world

Look to you

For leadership

To eliminate urban pollution

And combat climate change

To work with science

For a better world

Do not betray us

San Francisco

By investing in

Our own deceit

The Comedians

The comedians are arrested

Tortured

And incarcerated

In

Egypt

Burma

Tunisia

Tibet

For poking fun

At governments

Humor

An antidote

For oppression

Loss of freedom

The best antidote

For criticism

Of any government

Is crushed

But never

Destroyed

Violence Again

Violence again
Boston after Newton
After drones and before drones
And bombs
In Afghanistan
Palestine
Targeting populations
Violence which begets
Violence
Terrorism
Yes, all violence
Seeds and breeds
Terror
Drones,
Napalm
Guns
Bombs
And violence
Against nature
Agent Orange
Depleted uranium
Toxic waste
Violence
Bullying
Ignoring
Torturing
Let San Francisco
Take a stand
Against all violence
Especially that
Of our own nation

Caveat Populus (The Living Wage comes riding on a horse)

Cinco de Mayo begins in Puebla, Mexico 1862

The French are routed

The election of President Benito Juarez

Reinstalls democracy

Cinco de Mayo

Let democracy run free

Let democracy be of and for the people

Equity in wages

Equity in health

Equity in education

Equus

To afford a horse

Means to be obliged

In Rome

The business man

Who owns a horse

Owns status

And is obliged

Noblesse oblige

Equus demands

Equity for the cavalier

The rider of horses

And the people

Caveat

Always a caveat

Caveat emptor

The buyer takes the risk

Caveat

Cavalier Equity becomes

Entitlement

Entitlement

Belongs not to the cavalier

But to the people and the land

Caveat populus

The living wage comes riding on a horse

Demanding equity

Equus shall be equity for all

A living wage for all

Caveat Equus

Let democracy run free

Let democracy come riding

Of and for the people

Equus populus

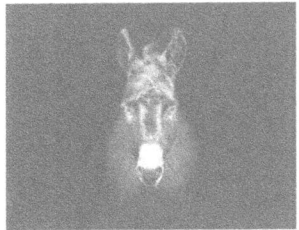

Seventh Ward New Orleans Mother's Day

Nineteen people injured in a Mother's Day Parade
New Orleans, Seventh Ward, May 2013
Children, adults, hurt by three gunmen
Shooting at their own lives
Shooting at their own communities
Shooting at their families
Their hopes
Their future
Seventh Ward was a vibrant community
Birthplace to musicians, majors, artists, writers
Jelly Roll Martin called the Seventh Ward home
Barney Bigard and Sidney Bechet and Frank Ocean
The producer Mannie Fresh
And rappers Miz X and MC L
Civil rights leader A.P. Tureaud
And playwright Tyler Perry
Authors Fatima Shaik and Mona Lisa Saloy
Names that roll off the tongue and scream out
We lived here! We created here! This is our birthplace!
Their home is now singing
 With yellow flowers
Creeping out of attics and through slats of floors
Up through abandoned pavements
Yellow flowers
Taking possession of homes
As proxies for the banks who have foreclosed
On Katrina's victims
Who could not pay mortgage
On flooded homes
Who could not repair
Broken pipes
Broken lives
Broken dreams

Serves them right
Cries a voice from the bank
They didn't buy insurance
Seventh Ward
Forgotten
Like the wild dogs
Dying of abandonment
Prowling their grief
Serves them right
Victims of cracked levies
Drowned, dead
Or abandoned
To the creeping
Yellow flowers
Surrounding
Their ancestral
Homes
Three respond
Like the cracked levies
Their Cracked lives
Cracked with cocaine
And desperation
Crack rifles
And shoot
Desperately
At yellow flowers

Artificial Turf Crowds out the Living World

Plastic aromas instead of grass
Polycarbonates and Bisphenol-A
Proven to interrupt endocrine cycles
Proven to affect fertility
Proven to lead to lower intelligence in developing brains
Now ever more popular on sports fields
And soon Golden Gate Park
San Francisco's oasis of green
Its sacred, natural sanctuary
Soon to be home to polluting esters from fake grass
To be played upon, rolled upon, wrestled upon
By children playing soccer or other sports
To gradually disintegrate as plastics do
And in the disintegration produce more pollutants
To invade growing brains
To invade growing bodies
Produce more pollutants from plastics
Made from fossil fuels
Plastics that are not bio-degradable
Plastics that disintegrate into bits of plastic
To be eaten by animals and birds
And find their way through the food chain
To us and our children
Polluting the bodies of animals and birds
And humans
Artificial turf
Is no proxy
For living growing green
Is no proxy
For life

Lights Beneath the Fog

Lights beneath the fog

Seem like torches

Consumed to burn away

The roof of clouds

And yet

Foggy softness

Turns to gray

And densely

Covers

All illumination

In the night

The city sleeps

And dreams

Of day

The Story of the Kikiyu

Twenty thousand Kikiyu
Killed or "disappeared"
Tortured, raped, castrated with pliers
Fetuses destroyed with glass bottles
Machine gun against sword
As colonialists
Helped themselves to land
Fecund land of the ancestral tribes
Pristine, productive,
Fed by clean water
Stolen from its owners
Called the Mau Mau
By colonialists
Who would prefer to eradicate the tribes
To eradicate the civilization
Of the Kikuyu of Kenya
Today tribes seek justice
For the wrongs
Perpetrated 65 years ago
Today indigenous peoples
Demand that the story be told
Demand the respect
Due their tribes and people
Demand answers
Demand their land
Once upon a time
Ugai itha began the stories of the Kikuyu
Rukirika ends the tale
Once a tribe of peace
Violated by colonial arrogance
Now a tribe whose story
Demands to be told

Scars of Global Repression

As repression screams with outrage
Bloodying our brains with open fangs
Venom spills into the human spirit
Curdling a soul with anguish
The snake writhes in our mind
Demanding justice
The snake propels us to the streets
To cry out against spies
To cry out against drones
To cry out against the destruction of our planet
To cry out against drilling into her heart
The heart of mother earth
Drilling, cutting ravaging the earth
For oil
For gas
Leaving scars in her body
That kisses
Cannot repair
In Turkey, a disenfranchised people
Take to the streets to demand a voice
To demand their legacy of freedom
To demand equal rights
To demand democracy
A constitution based on democratic ideals
A country that does not lock its women
Below deck
On ships that sink
And children and women
Die
Locked below deck
To protect their modesty
And assure their death

In Turkey, land of the library of Ephesus
Land of philosophers and poets
Land of universal health care
In ancient Asclepius
Universal
Except for the poor
In Turkey
Now tens of thousands throng
To defend their park
To protect Gezi Park
From destruction for a shopping mall
To protect a small piece of nature
Against a tyrant's exploitation
To protect their own freedoms
Against a government's greed
Turkey is no stranger to repression
The world does not forget Armenian genocide
Nor do the Kurds accept their own
Disenfranchisement
In Turkey,
Land of Cappadocia
Where persecuted peoples hid
In surreal caves
To nurture new ideas
And now today
In Turkey
People throng
To protect a park
And are set upon
By police, tear gas
And bullets
In Turkey an apology
For tyranny against the people
Will not suffice

In Hungary, the Roma children
Walk to the river Danube
With their parents
To throw flowers
Across the rusting, metal shoes
They cry bitter tears
Tears for the Jewish children and mothers
Asked to remove their shoes
Before being drowned in the river
Seventy years ago
The Roma gypsies and the Jews
Are again targets
For hatred and murder
In just ten minutes
A law was passed
Making it illegal
For homeless people
To loiter in public places
Where shall they go?
Poverty is not popular
It can also be lethal
In Hungary today

Poverty is not popular
In San Francisco
But lives upon its streets
In solidarity with the oppressed
Of Turkey and Hungary
Nourished by the venom
Of inequality
The venom of trauma
From wars and violence
Of corporations
Corporations

Exacting tribute
From war
Exacting tribute
From the land
Once held sacred
By the people
The people
Now forced to witness
The torture of their land
Through fracturing for gas and oil
Now forced to inhabit
Polluted plains and valleys
Once pristine with countless birds and animals
Pristine with countless species of flora and fauna
Pristine with unearthly and yet earthly beauty
The people grieve
The snake of justice
Screams with outrage
Bloodying our brains with open fangs
Venom spills into the human spirit
Curdling a soul with anguish
The snake writhes in our mind
Demanding justice
The snake propels us to the streets
To cry out against spies
To cry out against drones
To cry out against all repression
The repression of the human spirit
The repression of the mind
The repression of the body
The repression of the people
To cry out against the destruction of our planet
To cry out against drilling into her heart
The heart of mother earth

Drilling, cutting ravaging the earth
For oil
For gas
For corporations
Taking a piece of the flesh
Of earth
Taking a piece of the flesh
Of the people
Leaving scars in her body
That kisses
Cannot repair

The Standing Man   *- After police broke up the* protests *in*
Turkey's Taksim Square, a new protest *began—this one silent*

A man stands for justice
Not metaphorically
With his vote
Not with his written manifest
His life witness
Or as a mascot of peace
He stands
Because the government of Turkey
Says he may stand
To protest that government
If he does not interfere with traffic
So he stands to repudiate the government
He stands silently
He is careful not to interfere with traffic
Passersby raid his back pack
Laugh at him
Call him names
Others stand by his side
Stand with him
To stand against the greed of government
Stand for human rights
Not metaphorically
But physically
With their bodies they stand
Across the world
Other people go out into the streets
To stand for justice
Silently
Quietly
They stand
With the
Standing man
They stand
For justice

Tenderness is a Bridge

Tenderness is a bridge
A span from here to here
From heart to heart
From mind to thought
Girded with steel
So gentleness may find its way
Swinging on solid struts
Tenderness is a river
Flowing from here to here
From spirit to soul
From idea to embrace
Sweeping under rocks
Resting among mangroves
Playing with fiddler crabs
On its way to the sea
Tenderness is the sea
Rocked by the wind
Churning in the primal surf
Of lost consciousness
Luminescent in the sun's delicate first rays
Or radiant in its evening glory
Following the path from here to here
Across a glass fabric
Leading
To eternity

Children Wander the World

Children wander the world
Children without countries
Children without families
Children seeking homes
Seeking food
Seeking shelter
Twenty million children
Wander the world
Refugees
Homeless
Unrecognized numbers
Unaware of their birth dates
Unnamed
Empty of memories
That belong to childhood
Empty of belonging
Longing for memories
Of home
Unaware of childhood
Unaware of playtime
Running in garbage lots
To collect scraps
Not for toys
But for money
Not for themselves
But for bribes to survive childhood
The children
Come from disintegrating states
Whose names change with politics
Whose disintegration proceeds
Under their feet
Under their small bodies

Where corruption
Precedes terror
And terror
Precedes rape
Of young girls
Precedes conscription
Of young boys
Seven year old children
And younger
Wander through waste
Wander in terror
Orphans of AIDS and war
Nationless
I have seen them
Riding the trains
In India
Children
Tiny bodies
Scrambling down
The steps of trains
To wander again
To wander into our hearts
Where they remain alone
Where our hearts cannot gird them
Cannot clothe them
Cannot mitigate
The terror
Cannot mitigate
The hunger
Cannot mitigate
The longing
Of twenty million children

The Fog on Tuesday Night in July

The fog hides impending sunset

Humid and opaque

Rolling along the horizon

Soft, grey, silver screens

Glow gently from the sun's last sigh

Dispersing yawns

From foggy watercolor mouths

Washed in cool moisture

Blowing dense fog rings

Upward into the starless sky

Where genies catch

The fading circles

And cover

All the blue

Youth of the Moon

The moon has become agitated

Thinks her youth should be celebrated

She's much younger than 4 and a half billion

Take away at least 85 million

A few years here or there

Seems she's got them to spare

Now who says youth is so overrated!

Hibachi Birthday Party

He flexes his tools

Spinning

Tapping

Hammering

Throwing

Thrusting

Cutting on the hot surface

Of the hibachi

Mesmerizing his hungry audience

With ancient culinary acrobatics

Tossing with elegance

Eggs into his long red hat

A Latino practices

The magnificent art

Of the Japanese grill

With perfect skill and delight

Latino becomes Japanese

Becomes

Bulgarian, German

Swedish, American

Becomes

Everyone

Enjoying

Culinary delights

From the Hibachi grill

Malala Day

Remember the 15 year old girl

Malala Yousafzai

Shot in the head by the Taliban

Because she argued

Publically

In Pakistan

That all girls

All children

Have the right to education

Nine months later

The United Nations

Asks her to speak for education

Malala Day will be celebrated

She will ask that we use pens and paper

As our most effective weapons for peace

And yet

Many young girls

Who want to go to school

Will stay home

Because

Their fathers

Do not want them

To become

The next

Malalas

Malala shunned

Remember Malala
A teenage girl
Shot by the Taliban
For speaking out
For education for girls
In Pakistan
In Swat she is now reviled
She has made life dangerous
For other girls
Girls are afraid
To show sympathy
For Malala
For fear they or their families
Will be shot
Like Malala
She was a hero
Nominated for the
Nobel Prize
Now they call her
A pawn of the West
For being shot by the Taliban
And called a hero
Malala would like
To be prime minister
And fight for education

For all girls

So they will not be afraid

To speak up

So they will not be afraid

To be educated

Malala met with President Obama

And asked him to

Stop terrorizing people and nations

With drones

She asked him to focus on education

So people

In Pakistan

And everywhere

Will not be afraid

To ask for an end

To drones

And terror

Will not be afraid

To ask for education

Will not be afraid

To speak to Malala

San Francisco Scents

I walk towards the wharf
Enveloped in scents
I walk past bougainvillea, lilies
Clusters of opening blossoms
Exuding tropical dreams
Wrapped up in coffee
Spiced with dog smells
On the corner near Trader Joe's
The unmistakable
Pungency of marijuana lingers
San Francisco scents
Follow me to the fishermen
Rinsing their catch
Find me wrapping aromas
Around halibut
Lying flat within their square tank
Offering one last breath
Of ocean perfume
To a bouquet of scents
Brushing past me
In the breeze
Brushing past me
In the wind
Exhaling smells of freedom
In San Francisco

A Boy Killed

A boy was killed
In Florida
For being black
And young
Carrying candy
In his pocket
An unarmed boy
Was killed
In Florida
For being
Seventeen
And black
Carrying candy
Black children
Now carry signs asking
Am I next?
A boy was killed
By a man with a gun
By a man
With impunity in his pocket
A boy was killed
For being
Black
And young

His name was Martin

The ark of the moral universe

Bent far too wide

Bent over the entire world

But did not bathe

This boy in light

Did not bathe

This boy with justice

A bullet of historical bigotry

A bullet of hate and arrogance

Entered a young boy's body

And pierced his world

In bitter tears

And pierced his world

In the blood of injustice

The ark of the moral universe

Described once by another Martin

A Martin with a dream

To heal the world

Bent far too wide

Bent far too long

To save Trayvon Martin

A young

Black boy

With candy

In his pocket

Thoughts on Light and Openness

Wormwood
Burrows
Walking in the woods
Transparency
Safety is in the imagination
Equal freedom to see and hear
To communicate infinitely
Openly
Transparency is comfort
Security like a baby's
Security blanket,
Love, warmth, knowledge, trust
Total openness abnegates spying
There is no need
A light shines in the street
Evening
Shines brightly
Under speckled lights
Of windows along the hill
Tracing a path of bright spots
Up to Coit Tower
Perched as a sentinel
Warmly lit
Above the brilliant
Streetlight on Mason and Chestnut
Streetlights at night
Echo the moon
On moonlit evenings
Nature and urbanity
Vie for the light
Nothing is hidden
In spite of the dark of night

The Disappeared Women

Sixty million

Girls

Women

Have been raped

And murdered in India

They call them

"Disappeared"

In Asia in 2001

The estimate was

One hundred million

Women

Missing

Murdered

Disappeared

The birthrate

For girls

Keeps falling

Girls are unwanted

They are expensive

As brides

And useful

Only

As servants

Or victims

Of murder

Girls may be aborted

They may be neglected

Or ignored as babies

Or killed by their husbands

If the dowry is insufficient

Female tourists shun India

After the gang rape

Of a girl in a bus

Battered by a bar

And raped

By a gang of men

Then left by the side of

The road

To die

Of internal

Injuries

And yet

Every minute

Women are raped

And murdered

Girl babies

Are aborted

And men

Cannot make brides

Of dead

Women

A Child's Death by Drone

In Yemen

Drones killed

An enemy

Yesterday

They say

Drones

Killed children

Yesterday

We know

A father mourns

His eight-year- old

Daughter

Her death

Is not balanced

By the loss of

An enemy

But compounds

The tragedy

Of murder

All life is sacred

Drones are

Murderers

Of sacred

Life

Let us Close the Book of War

Let us close the book of war
Let us burn it in the oil of genocide
That those who died
Might rise from its ashes
Like the legendary Phoenix
To recreate love
Let us close the book of war
Let us drown it
In the tears of all the children
In the blood of all those massacred
That they might wash up again
On the shores of a new world
To recreate beauty
Let us close the book of war
Let us bury it
In the fields of war
Beneath all those slain
Beneath the cries of pain
Beneath the rocks
And fire
And water of earth
Let us close the book of war
Destroy its horror
And wrap cool earth
Around the fragments
Of its pages
That earth and fire and water
Might transform
The book of war
Into regenerated
New beginnings
Of love and peace

The Prisoners Starve Themselves

The prisoners starve themselves
In Pelican Bay
And Guantanamo
It is their only power
The power to disempower
Their own bodies
To let their bodies shrivel from hunger
As a cry for justice
How long, cry their bodies
How long will we submit
To humiliation
For crimes committed as a child
Or crimes committed as a soldier
For crimes never voiced
Never tried by Constitutional right
Of Habeas Corpus
For crimes unnamed
For crimes assumed
And never named
Or no crimes at all
What use to the soul and society
Is my body
In solitary confinement
To prevent my body
Perhaps
From strangling itself
My body says it will starve
To be in control of one aspect
Of its being
My body says it will refuse
To nourish itself
For further exploitation
And humiliation

After a Meteor Shower in San Francisco

Last night the sky
Was full of stars
Someone could see
Somewhere
Our sky was blanketed
With fog
Between our eyes
And the stars
Eons of time and miles
Separated us
From the stars
Behind the fog
Last night
The meteors were dancing
Line dancing in columns
Of meteor showers
Behind the fog
We could not see them
But I could hear them
Dancing

Humboldt Jetties

South and north

Stretching across the horizon

Home to mussels, pelicans

Nursery to fish and algae

Doing battle with ten foot waves

Crashing

Then eddying in swirling gasps

The head at the north

Hosting a lighthouse warning

To all who come close

We venture near

To admire

And then gaze

At the ancient

Undying

Sea

129

Hunger and Climate

More than three million children
Die each year of malnutrition
Or, simply, hunger
Poor people suffer most
And yet when surfeits of grain
Flood their countries
The farmers cannot sell their produce
And cannot feed their children
Climate change sends floods
And drought
Migratory birds
Arrive from their journeys
Famished
To find their food
Has vanished
Or gone north
To cooler climates
Terns no longer find herring
For their young
The large butterfish they offer
Cannot fit the tiny beaks
Of their starving hatchlings
Who perish
Never to sing or soar
Lost forever
And we too hunger
For lost beauty
While three million
Children die
Who will never again
See a bird in flight
Nor hear its song

Political Musings on Government Spying

The curtain of deception
Duplicity
Betrayal
Of CSC
Could have been raised earlier
Before one man
Had the courage
To risk his job and life
To expose the stage of spies
Spies that infiltrate our lives
Spies that send prisoners abroad
To be tortured
Or like Al-Mosri
Abducted and tortured
On a plane in free skies
Spies to hide atrocities
Committed by US troops
Spies to deceive investors
With irregular accounting
Spread across continents
Computer Science Corp
Sounds innocuous
Technical
Efficient
Remains a metaphor for rot and fraud
According to the British
Sued by its own stockholders
CSC smears obfuscates and ignores
Our Fourth Amendment
CSC sees all
Betrays all
The curtain has been raised

So we may see as well
Keep the curtain high
Keep the stage lit
Keep the spotlights bright
On every actor scurrying
For the shadows

(The CSC/Computer Science Corp runs NSA's internal IT system, allegedly making millions as contractor for the world's largest surveillance system: see CSCfraud.com)

Trans-Pacific Partnership

Trans-Pacific Partnership
Rings and sings like community family
Global peace
Friendship love mutuality
Fascism clothed in the robes of democracy
Corporate hegemony painted with the brush
Of partnership
Slave labor overseas disguised as jobs for all
Rights for banks to write their rules
Developers to ignore the environment
Governments to sneeze at climate change
Industries to muzzle invention
Trans-Pacific Partnership
Singing a smug song of support
For the citizens of the world
Singing a song
Of a new world order
A new and better WTO
A World Trade Organization
With sharper teeth
And stronger jaws
Framing an open mouth
Prepared to swallow
A tender pulsing world
In a feeding frenzy

I am not Indifferent

The breeze blows softly on my face
Escaping to race across the waves
Of the blue bay
Not really blue
Rather reflecting grey yellow cloud shadows
Floating in rippling measure
To the sounds of a saxophone
I wonder if we ruin the scene
With our chain link fences
Concrete, macadam
Funny casual clothes
Around the corner
Michael Jackson lives again
White face
Gloved hand
Funky steps and spins
The breeze captures him too
The breeze and the bay
Are indifferent to the dance
Indifferent to the clothes
Indifferent to the man in a wheelchair
Indifferent to the girl in rolling healed sneakers
Indifferent to me
But I am not indifferent
To the gull standing serenely
On the rail overlooking the bay
Her feathers gently ruffling
Or the sea lion barking at the moving clouds
Or the man in a wheelchair
Gazing across the grey green waves
Or the girl rolling by
Laughing at the breeze

Monterey Bay Beneath the Surface

Beneath the bay in Monterey

Beneath the flowing tide

Beneath sun sparkled surface of the water

Beneath the sunbaked rocks

Where seabirds and mammals loll

Lie beds of multi-colored kelp

Rippling and flowing over

Five pronged sea stars

Walking on tiny tubular sneakers

Orange and yellow sunflower sea stars

With multiple appendages

Darting tiny fish

Small sand dollars

Patient large rocks

Allowing populations

Of plants and sea creatures

To cling to its surface

Creating pastel masterpieces

Beneath the surface of the bay

Beneath the wind in Monterey

Beneath another breathing world

The salty water bearing ancient witness

To the hulls of seagoing vessels

Creating history above the surface

Of the bay in Monterey

Terror walks the Streets

Terror walks the streets

She who was born in vengeance

Memory her mother

Delivered eternally in loss

Suckled with the blood

Of fallen angels

Wrapped in sorrow

Rocked in grief

Cradled in steel arms

Of cold and bitter memory

Raised in desecrated

Fields of war's debris

Nurtured with the stories

Of ancestral wrongs

Of holocausts

And hatred

Terror is the child

Who screams

For retribution

And finds no solace

In the brush

Of wings

Upon her soft

And yielding cheeks

A Prayer for the Girls of Abuja

A prayer bursts through my brain

Cutting through stars

Piercing clouds and sunrise

Chopping rainbows into pieces

Kaleidoscopic pain of young girls

Two scrambling in bushes of Abuja

Hiding among limbs and brambles

Now damp with tears

Hiding as the truck

They escaped

Rambles by

Full of young girls' dreams

A burned school

Burning hate

Blinding the eyes

Of young girls crowded in a truck

Now damp with tears

Trucks scream by

One hundred twenty-nine young girls

Girded only with pieces

Of rainbow

(April 14, in Abuja, Nigeria, Boko Haram, whose name means, according to Al Jazeera, "Western education is forbidden", set off a bomb on the outskirts of Abujaba which killed 75 people, then abducted 129 Chibok schoolgirls, ages 15-18 from their school; fears remain of a similar situation to that of Uganda's Lord's Resistance Army, which abducted thousands of school-aged girls across central Africa to use as forced "wives" for their commanders)

Hegemony

Hegemony of nations
Manifest destiny
Ego of exceptionalism
Spells auto-annihilation
The human species
Wraps the world
In a shroud
Dyed in greenhouse gases
Sewn with carcinogens
Adeptly
Expertly stitched
With needles of war
Spun from looms of
Capitalism
Spinning wheels
Spinning nature into death
Cassandra cries, "Halt halt"
Reverse the wheel
Walk through the mirror
Unroll the shroud
Pay homage to nature
That she may create
The hegemony of exigency
The hegemony
Of all life regenerated
Shred the corrupting rags
Strangling earth
Roll back the last sunset
Glowing with our own hell
Of domination
That a pristine dawn may rise
With gentle justice

Fuzzy Green Things

Fuzzy green things
Slide inexorably
From a moist
Earthen domain
Knowing intuitively
Their time is come
To regenerate
To thrust themselves
And wind and curl
Explode
Unwrap
Lie naked
Clothing the earth
In their nakedness
Seeking warmth and light
Opening themselves
Unashamedly
To the sun's embrace
Performing coital rituals
To conceive new forms
To fulfill the
Manifest destiny
Of nature
To hybridize
Errant offspring
Inseminate
Corrupt flesh
With chaste seed
Springtime after springtime
Until purity
Inevitably
Returns

Springtime's Regeneration

Springtime's regeneration
Does not compete with global errors
Made manifest by human excess
And burned forests
Springtime rises and thrusts
Above corruption
Into a spirit world
Where social ills are moot
Human creatures scurry to offer
Alms to nature
Rites of violence
Creeds of capitalistic fervor
Clutching, claiming and destroying
The very gifts of nature
She offers back with open arms
Her children know best how to take
And to abuse
Yet as all earthly mothers
Nature forgives
And wraps her creatures
Again in arms of grace
Suckles greedy mouths
And offers them
With raised arms
To the light

Round-Up Ready

Suicides by farmers

270,000 and rising

Their families starve

As they are forced off their farms

By the scourge of Monsanto

Doctors say babies are dying

Childhood cancer is soaring

Parallel with the success of Monsanto

The modified seeds are Round-Up ready

Round-Up

Infamous herbicide

Killer of fertile humus

Killer of venerable old heirloom seeds

Round-Up ready

Ready to dominate all seeds and weeds

Who succumb to Round-Up

Ready to be corralled into genetic servitude

Are we unmodified human creatures

Ready to be modified?

Ready to be round up?

Ready to die

If we are not Round-Up ready?

Or ready to sacrifice our children

To a Round-Up ready world?

I saw the Moon Last Night

I saw the moon last night

Hanging suspended

Between Coit Tower

And Saints Peter and Paul

As I walked up Mason Street

In San Francisco

Just hanging there

Looking sovereign and perplexed

Transparent and opaque

Giving the distinct impression

She would be ready

To hold court with earth

Knowing she is an unequal partner

Just a satellite

Yet charged with the timing of tides

The magnetic pull of continents and oceans

Regarded as muse of poets

Icon of harvest

Catalyst of romance

I saw the moon last night

Shining over our world

Sailing through a twilight sky

Then on through darkness

One Wheel

One wheel of a bicycle

Stands silently

Before the window

Waiting for someone

To sit and make the pedals move

Against its frame

Waiting for motion

For energy

On its bars hang

Laundry items

Still drying

Jeans and a folded

Pair of pants on its seat

Possibly

Already

Dry

Waiting

For company

Delray Beach, Florida

The sand is white
The water warm
Pelicans and small birds
Dive, skim the glassy sea
Catch the tiny silver fish
That jump through glass
Sliding from their ocean home
Into a world of sun
And an intrepid
Beak

A Dog Barks

A dog barks into the night
The same dog perhaps
Who barked this morning
A new dog in the neighborhood
Sending his or her bark
Into the wilderness
Of city streets
Asking only that someone
Pay attention

An Ant

An ant looks neither up nor down

What purpose such glances

To an ant

Informed by sweet

Or bitter

By textures

Grainy silky clinging

Slippery muddy

Wet

Dry

Envelopes of space

Or freedom

Paper cardboard cloth

Ceramic tile

Wooden slats

Bark

Informed by meetings

With mammals reptiles

Plants insects

Devoured

Or finding tenderness

In the company

Of another

Ant

Kofi Awoonor Dies in Kenya

A poet died in Nairobi
In a mall
Westgate Mall
September 21, 2013
Senseless
As death can be
His son
Shot by his side
Survived
Kofi Awoonor
Had written
Poetry and prose
From a profound heart
And a brilliant mind
He was 78
Born in 1935 in Ghana
In 1935 the drumbeats
To another war
May have shaken his cradle
He named his daughter
The Human Being
He was imprisoned
For saving another
From greater injustice
His poetry was gentle
As his life was meant to be
He was Ambassador
To the United Nations from Ghana
He will be remembered as a poet
Killed senselessly in a shopping mall in Kenya
By a gun
That stopped the music

The Atlantic Stretches Southward

The Atlantic stretches southward

Towards the Caribbean

Infinitely

Water into water

Cloud into cloud

Bird cry into bird cry

Granite sandy bottoms

Subsiding into

Coral reefs

Becoming

Calcium carbonate sands

Disgorged by

Multi-colored tropical fish

Chewing on coral masterpieces

My Grandson loves to Fold Laundry

My grandson is nearly ten

And loves order

He will organize

The laundry

With patience

Sock after sock

And would iron them

As well

If his mother

My daughter

Would let him

The laundry rises

In baskets

Like leavened bread

Folded towel

After folded towel

Rising toward

The basement ceiling

Until a voice calls

Behind the rising bread

Of laundry

Mommy,

We need to

Wash more clothes!

Cruise to the Caribbean

A ship sails southeast

Housing five thousand people

A small village riding on a boat

A crew from one hundred different countries

Creating a mini United Nations

To care for

Retired vacationing

People children families

Playing

Dancing

Eating

Sometimes overindulging

Old young happy despairing

Vulnerable invulnerable

Escaping enjoying

Watching the sea

Sailing southward

Unaware of a lurking pandemic

Soon to stop the party

The Dragon that Can

The NSA system in Utah is down
Like a dragon in a cave
Choking on its own fire
Health Care in America
Excludes its poorest citizens
The cooks, cleaners and nurses' aides
The children in the Deep South
Are too poor to qualify
Their states can deny them
Doctors, hospitals and medicine
Because our nation's lawmakers
Say they can
Our government refuses to help
The poorest states with the poorest people
California has the power to influence movement
Towards a federal mandate
That all be covered regardless of
The impoverishment of
The states where they live
Let us be the dragon that could
Let California become the magic dragon
That demands justice
Let San Francisco become the dragon
That demands that our state demand of our nation
The right to health care
For all who live
In this great country
Let the NSA dragon
Choke on its own fire
While the monies spent feeding it
Be spent to save the lives
Of the poorest of the poor

Death in Arizona

It wasn't a gated community
The people in Glen Llah and Yarnell
In Arizona
Had incomes of about $24,000 a year
Maybe less
Their homes were average
Nice homes with gardens
And shrubs and brush and dry grass
And fire prone manzanita
Some said their homes were surrounded
With the equivalent
Of 50,000 gallons of gasoline
Where firefighters fought in vain
To save a community
Hit by lightning
Where nineteen firefighters died
When the wind changed
Nineteen ace firefighters died
Saving property
Leaving bereft families
And children
Because a community
In Arizona
Did not clear the brush

A Body is Found

A body is found
Three weeks dead
Found on a back stairway
In a hospital
Maybe that of a woman
Admitted to the hospital
Three weeks ago
Maybe not
Buildings now have no escape mechanisms
Walk down a stairway
In a residential building
Or a hospital
And you may be unable to return
Through the door you just closed
For the security of the building
Security from you
Walk down the stairs
Of a hotel
Walk through a door
At the bottom of the stairs
Let the door close
It will lock behind you
To secure the building
From you
And no one
May hear your knocking
Or hear
Your cries of help
Security is for buildings
Not for you
Or the body just found
At General Hospital
San Francisco

More Factories Burn in Bangladesh

More workers died yesterday

In Bangladesh

As if one thousand deaths

Were not enough

For Gap and Walmart

To insist the factories

In Bangladesh

Be closed

Until they were safe

Be closed

Until the workers are safe

Be closed until the children

Are sent to school

With funds from Walmart and Gap

Until the littlest ones

Are placed in safe child care

With funds from Gap and Walmart

Near where their parents work

In safe conditions

In factories that will not burn

That will not implode

That will not kill children

In factories that will not kill

Parents, sisters, brothers, uncles, aunts, grandparents

In factories that will not kill

The Dish and the Spoon of the Moon

The spoon of the moon
Let Venus slip into the heavens
She rolled away into the dark sky
Laughing back at the spoon
Glowing against an enormous
Dish of the sky

Home in a Van

He sits in his van
Weathered and bearded
"Goin' fishin"
Is sprayed
Across the sides of the van
Against a bright, multi-colored
Graffiti-emulating backdrop
He sits there
Days on end
Observing the world
Walking by

Flies Live Long Lives

I read that flies

Live long lives

Experiencing each moment

In slow motion

They live in

Macro time

Washing their faces

For days

As we observe

Their flickering arms

Rubbing

As our seconds

Tick by

I imagine giants

Watching us

From some enormous

Chair in the sky

Seeing our peregrinations

Around this small planet

As a miniscule

Afterthought

Government Shuts Down Vermeer

The last time the government shut down
I had just come back from France
Having seen Vermeer in Bordeaux
The exhibit had come to the Smithsonian
Miles of people waiting to see Vermeer
Stretched around the mall
Waiting in vain
To see the great Dutch painter
Master of quiet moments
Master of detail
Master of perspective
Now missing
In Washington

Masts in the Harbor

Masts sway
In varied rhythms
A slow waltz
A lullaby
A two-step with no partner
The masts all dance solo
Against a blue white sky
Solo in their rhythms
Blending solo
Sway ensemble
Anchored to
Reflected rope
Strands
Creating triangles
Upon water
Under stationary carriages
Dancing upon magic hooves
Dappling the rippling
And green dance floor
Dancing to the rhythms
Of their solo shadows
Creaking
Among triangles
Of rope

The Sky is Blue

The sky is totally blue today
No sign of clouds or moon
They are hiding perhaps
Tucked behind the mirror of day
Reflecting a sky
Totally blue

Hotel Room by the Bay

The shadows
Dapple ceiling and wall
Etched through the silken curtains
Reflected in the mirror
Etchings describe
Ridges and rivulets of sand
Under the waters of the bay

October's Moon

The nearly full moon sails upon pale blue
Shrouded by the veil of Venus
The eastern sky
Ethereal
The west
Glowing softly
The fading sun
Tips its golden cap
To an amorous
Yet distant
Moon

Impressionism at Twilight

Upon a rippling bay
Dappled with red green purple
Luminescence
Brushes dip into
The palette of the sun
Rolling her golden carpet
Over a rainbow sea

Sand Mining

The unpriced cost of exploitation
Faced by every transformation
Sand from beach to concrete road
Loss of land with every load
Holes dug in our living room
The planet's space, the planet's doom
Water rising to our sheets
Becoming shrouds, the rising heat
Of water rising, rising on our home
Where we ourselves simply repeat
The never ending exploitation
Of our sandy sedimentation
Sand is gold and water silver
Sand and water are our treasure
Ours to guard
Measure for measure
Sand is silver, water gold
Beneath our feet
Repeat, repeat
The sandy song,
The water's sigh
A human touch
A soft goodbye

Tokyo Bay

Skyscrapers
White filtering masks on passengers
Four years old, a tiny face behind a mask,
Elastic strings tucked behind the ears
Smooth landing and the hustle of debarking
Immigration, taxis, friendly buses
Hotel on a hill
Dinner by pushing your choice, entering yen
Miso soup, noodles, beef, broccoli, rice
Laundry in the sink, hanging everywhere
Amid the humidity
Sweet sleep sumptuous breakfast
West and east combined
People
 Japan, India, Florida, California
Focusing on finding ways to heal the world
To heal the coast
To heal
Filtering ideas to breathe, to nourish
Filtering ideas to grow
People
Skyscrapers
Bay

Shrouds

Hectic this morning
After a cold night
Fog shrouding the bay
Glimpses of pale streets
Glowing from luminous
Street lights and windows
Veiled in fog
Hidden faces and dreams
Plunge from silent obscurity
Into the fray of shuttles
Trolleys street cars
Bay Area Rapid Transit
Breaks the union strike
Under another shroud
Of tragic error and death
A train too fast
A train no one expected to be there
A conductor being trained
To operate for striking
Union workers
Kills two contractors
Inspecting tracks for safety
On a day
The trains did not run

Sunday Afternoon in Portland

We played poker well sort of
My grandson played out all his chips
His friend gamely refereed
We figured out hold check
And mostly laughed
We played poker well sort of
They went to the park without lunch
They came back with potato chips
Sort of lunch
They went to my grandson's room
From the sound of it
Scrapings on the floor and bangs
They must have moved furniture
I see another child next door
Looking at a smartphone
Engrossed in a game perhaps
As her feet find steps
Going down she turns
Goes back into the house
The wind rustles the trees
The sun shines brightly
On a very green city
My daughter walks in with
A new toy for her son
A green laser beam
Life is not so different I imagine
From the time children played in the Stone Age
They just had different toys
They probably took them apart
The bones and sticks and piles of rocks
Gradually decimated like today's plastic toys
And their shiny electric components
Toys equally ephemeral a million years ago

Murder on Earth

London

Orlando

The killing continues

Hate or anger

Terrorism or revenge

What is seething in the human spirit

That boils over into murder?

Even the world is being slowly murdered

By hatred or indifference

And we watch and wring our hands

As our own government

Draws a veil over its responsibility

Walks away from agreements

To cease murdering the earth

We continue to drill into its heart

Continue to pollute its waters

Continue to kill its children

London and Orlando

Murder continues

While coral reefs shrivel

Under murderous acids

Marine life dies

While the earth responds

To human hate and terrorism

With acid tears

Solitude

Solitude
Like single drops of rain
Splash alone
Disintegrate
In blossoms of water
Wet petals
Etched on glass
Subsumed in earth
Slide on wet pavement
Drop again from damp leaves
Lose themselves
On the surface of oceans
In the maelstrom of waterfalls
In the turmoil of wind
Alone
Single
Yet absorbed
Again
By themselves
Speaking
Solitude

Earth Calls

Earth calls out
From her clouds and water
Her mudslides
Her timeless trees
Her jubilant saplings
And nesting birds
Her salmon swimming
Against currents to spawn again
Her deer rubbing off old antler hides
Discarding the old for the ever new
Nature calls out to humankind
You may use and abuse me
As a child will its parent
But I will endure
Do not fear my demise
My moon will rise
Perhaps millennia and more
My sun will soar
My love will fill your sleep
As nature always keep
You close
Until you choose to go
Your wounds upon my flesh
Will cause you suffering
And pain
Your arrows
Harm you only
As you aim
Into your heart
My own is yours
I will endure

Sunshine and Shelter

The windows and roofs of houses

March up the sunny hillside

Casting shadows

Yet sparkling

In afternoon sunshine

Beneath their shimmering glory

The city streets

Stretch out languidly

Receiving bundles of humanity

Under doorways

Next to curbs

In huddled spaces

Now tentless

Allowed to lie

But not seek cover

On languid city streets

Beneath

Sparkling homes

Reflecting sunshine

And shelter

Tents

Tonight

I walked to my car

On Larch Street

Off of Van Ness

Across the street

Tents had been put up

For shelter

And sleep

I had never seen tents

On Larch Street before

I wondered

How many other streets

Had become bedrooms

For the homeless

In San Francisco

I wondered

If the city

Would require

That the tents be removed

On Larch Street

And wherever

Tents

Are sheltering

Those who have

No shelter

Spooned Up

Runes ruminate

Dunes denigrate

Loons peregrinate

Boons

Goons

Buffoons

Soon

In tune

With a

Lunatic

Moon

Spooned up

From the soup

Of the sky

At the Coffee Shop

Two people talk about mothers
Daughters and friends
Indian and white wedding
White wedding?
How strange
Speaking of skin not gown
What is a white wedding?
She says it is the ritual
She kind of gets it
She says it is their choice
Not my wedding
A white wedding
The sky is blank
A blue canvas
Waiting to be painted
With clouds
White clouds
With airplanes
Now only buildings edge its frame
Cables stretch across the canvas
Dipping into human structures
From poles stretched high
Into indifferent space
Extra layers placed on earth
Intrude into blue
Suggesting invasion or harmony
Across the earth
Across wet blue
Under sky blue
Other continents
Scream with fire and agony
Painted with invasions of violence

Describing their layers
Of human intervention
The blue canvas of the sky
Is painted with sorrow
A brush extended over blue on blue
Sky on ocean
Extended over land
From land at peace
Painting war on other lands
While land and sea and shore
Remain indifferent
Wind and rain
Time and change
Restore their blue and brown and white
Seen from universes far beyond
A blue sphere
Indifferent to pain though wounded
Through apathy and greed
The sphere spins again and again
Waiting to be painted with birds or trees
Scenes of sunset sunrise
Dawn and dusk
And ordinary days
Or fiery hells of human excess
Waiting to be painted
Waiting for new shapes
To edge its frame
Waiting perhaps
For an Indian
White wedding
Or not
It is their choice

The Children are Hungry

Sixteen million children in the United States

Go to bed hungry

Twenty two million

Live in poverty

One in four of the world's children are stunted

By malnutrition

Sixty-six million primary school children

Go to class

Hungry

Try to learn to read

To do arithmetic

To break out of the cycle of poverty

But they are hungry

It is difficult to learn

When the body aches for food

Difficult to sleep

Difficult to play

Difficult to live

Difficult to be

A child

Difficult to be

At all

Difficult to be

Hungry

The Children After School

They come as the sun is setting

I wish my mommy would pick me up

I don't have a mommy

She didn't eat for a week

A sad gesture as the moon

Looks down on all the children

One in my arms

Who fell a moment ago

Navigating steps in the playground

He points his hand

At the moon

I need an ice pack

We go hand in hand

To the refrigerator

His mommy comes

Then disappears again

To fetch his backpack

He wonders

Where she is

And cradles

His ice on a damp face

Water is life

Water is sustenance
When water goes bad
When people in Texas, Pennsylvania and Wyoming
Complain that their drinking water
Bubbles
Smells
Can be lit with a match
When it is tested
And proven to contain
Methane
And arsenic
The EPA requests that
 Oil and Gas companies
Fracking companies
Investigate
Themselves
As they
Continue polluting
The water
Continue fracturing
For oil
Continue digging
For treasure
Continue failing
To treasure

Water

Continue failing

To treasure

Life

As they investigate

Their own corrupt

Practices

That they may continue

Polluting

Continue contaminating water

With impunity

1Texas: Complaints of water bubbling like champagne. But after Fracking Company Range Resources threatened not to participate in another study in March 2012, the EPA set aside the "smoking gun" report connecting methane migration to fracking.

2. Dimock, PA – The mid-Atlantic EPA began testing water in Dimock, PA after residents complained that their drinking water was contaminated from nearby fracking operations. But the federal EPA closed the investigation in July 2012 even after the staff members who had been testing the water warned of methane, manganese and arsenic contamination.

3. Pavilion, WY – The EPA released a draft report in 2011 linking fracking to contamination of an underground aquifer. After drawing criticism from the oil and gas industry, the EPA handed the investigation over to the state of Wyoming in June 2013 to be completed with funding from EnCana, the drilling company charged with contaminating the water wells in the first place

The Old Gibbous Moon

The old gibbous moon

Illuminated like a glowing lantern

Hangs over the night sky

Knowing its glow wanes

As sultry shadows

Edge into the light

Displacing moonbeams

The old gibbous moon

Smiles behind a veil of secrets

Sliding slowly through

A sea of darkness

Waning wordlessly

The old gibbous moon

Glides like a boat

Disappearing as it rolls through

The waters of the universe

Almost unnoticed

Across

Night waters

175

Sankofa Views

We live in timelessness

Like the bird Sankofa

Extending her neck across her back

To view her own ancestral abyss

Yet circling back as she walks forward

Past and present become future dreams

The child is father and mother

Of its own conception

Remembering a world within a womb

Where timelessness embraces time

And spirits rest in gardens

Of antiquity

Fecund until the end

And the beginning

Of all time

The Moon Explodes

The moon explodes

Her cradle rocking

Behind a shimmering

Exploding veil

Too brilliant to gaze upon

As if imitating the sun

For one bright moment

The Crime of Protest in Egypt

Twenty-one women form a human chain

To protest Egyptian laws banning protests

They are sentenced to eleven years in prison

One 19 year old girl phones her mother to say

I will be thirty when I get out of prison

I was not guilty of any charges

Except appearing in public to protest

To protest laws that say I cannot protest

None of us is guilty of any crime but loving Egypt

The Sun is Bright

The sun is bright and blinding in the December morning
Glaring unforgivably at human adventures under its light
Burning away all vestiges of fog
Nature has no secrets
Neither dissembles nor betrays
Transparent to the seeing eye
Pragmatic in its innocence
Gathering its storms
Releasing torrents
Making rivers seas floods
Deserts plains prairies tundra
Neither forgiving nor seeking forgiveness
As the world turns
The moon slides around its planet
And both circumnavigate
A blinding sun
Nature has no secrets
Is neither compassionate nor seeking compassion
Neither empathic nor seeking empathy
Exploding into fire, minerals, water and life
Life that becomes human
Life that seeks to dissemble
Seeks to lie
To hide
To cover secret paths and actions
Yet cannot contain
What it would seek to hide
Cannot contain
What nature has ordained
To be transparent
Under a blinding
Yet life-giving sun

The Christmas Season

The Christmas season dances into December

Elves propagate street corners

Trees shimmer in gowns of light and color

Babies reach out to a sparkling world

Songs remind us of another child

Still not forgotten after two thousand years

Whose tiny hands once reached out

To light the candles of Hanukkah

Who grew into a boy

Who argued with the rabbis

A man with the strong arms of a carpenter

Who preached upon a mountain

That love is stronger than hate

More powerful than power

More life giving than food or water

Needing no doctrine but embracing all ideas

That may be subsumed in love

The Christmas season dances into December

Innocence is caged in prisons

Waiting for love to unlock its doors

Worker's Budget

McDonalds teamed up with Visa

To create a budget

For a McDonald's worker

Assuming she worked two jobs

Paid $20 a month in health care

Nothing for heating

Or food

$600 for rent

And had $800

Left over

From $2060 a month

For two jobs

Average pay for

A McDonald's worker

Is $8.75 an hour

Its top CEO

Earns $825 million a year

A McDonald's executive

Takes home $25,000 each day

While another two-job worker

Scrubs off at his first McDonald's job

In the store bathroom

To be clean for the next McDonald's

So he won't lose his job

For smelling of grease

Ahmed Negm Dies in Cairo

Poet of the people
Who lamented
People care more about morality
Than dignity and life
More about unclothed women
Than the unclothed, under nourished
Who walk the streets of Cairo
Every day
Ahmed Negm
Another poet who was jailed
Like Ajami in Qatar*
For poetry
A poet with seventeen siblings
Raised in an orphanage
Who worked as a postman
And a house servant
Who inspired the revolution in 2011
Inspired the people
In Tahrir Square
With his songs
Accompanied by a blind oud player
Ahmed Negm wrote to his daughters
They might never brag
About their father
But they would never
Be ashamed of him
For that belief
He claimed
To have happily
Paid the price

*Mohammed al Ajami, student at Cairo University in 2011, was sentenced to
life imprisonment November 29, 2012 for poetry considered insulting to the
Emir; later the sentence was reduced to 15 years)

What is a Living Wage

What is a living wage?
What is justice?
I worked twelve hours a day
In Nantucket one summer
Opening and closing a shop
Nine to nine
For one dollar an hour
No breaks, no lunch
Sundays free
I slept on a broken cot
In the living room of a rental
Shared with four older girls
Who had beds
I had no idea
That was not fair
Yesterday a saw a man
Throw down his bag
In disgust
As a police car drove up
To take him away
Did he have a living wage?
Did he have a home?
Where do we find our dignity?
A key to unlock our own cages
Of disrespect?

Children should be taught

Self-dignity

Along with the multiplication tables

And spelling

The Constitution begins at home

And rights to life, liberty

And the pursuit of happiness

Children should be seen

And heard

Loved

And respected

The right to work

For fair wages

Imbedded in their sense of self

What is a living wage?

What is a living idea?

A living concept of self?

Tomorrow does not vacate today

But lives within this moment

Asking us

To unlock our freedom

To walk with dignity

To expect and anticipate justice

That it may one day

Become a reality

Icarus and Ison

Icarus flew too close to the sun

With wax wings from his father Daedalus

Curious and undeterred

He flapped on wingless arms

And fell into the sea

Ison, our new comet

Melted his fine wings

And flew into a universal sea

Let us mythicize them both

Let us eulogize them both

Partners of a questing gene

Philosophers upon their path

Of curiosity

We Walk Through Mirrors

We walk through mirrors

Life reflects our path in myriad pieces

The kaleidoscope turns

In never repeating designs

Bright and edgy

Moments of our journey

Swing in patterns

Through our space of joy and tears

184

Melted Truth

How different is real

From unreal

Phony from genuine

Sincere from insincere

Is truth consistent

When each person

Tells a different story?

I think the stories

Every version of

A real event

Or once upon a time

Should gather together

At a campfire one night

Singing songs

Close together

Close to the campfire

Closer still

Until they all melt

Into one truth

And yet

One melted truth

Would not be

Half as interesting

As unmelted lies

The Wind Unspeakably Proud

The wind

Unspeakably proud

Blows away houses boats

People animals

Leaving rags

Vestiges of civilization

And life

The wind

Unspeakably proud

Blows away

The world of human endeavor

Blows upon battle fields

Upon schools

Upon shops

Blows upon the poor

Mercilessly

Upon the rich

Equally

Disinterested in property

Or lives

Blows upon trees and

Dandelions

Who genuflect

Before the proud

Unspeakably proud

Wind

Who puffs and blows

Until all bow

Before its passage

Pausing to allow

The prideful wind

To pass

Until the aftermath

Of sweeping cloak and train

Gives pause enough for all

Gives time enough

For all to readjust

To realign

Resuscitate

Regenerate

Yet shaking off its drops

Even the dandelion

Is silent

As the wind

Unspeakably proud

Insufferably proud

Stops silently in awe

Drops cloak and train

In awe

Drops pride and power in awe

Of a rainbow

Mexico, land of flowers

Mexico, from the Pacific to the Gulf

Tijuana to Cabo San Lucas or

Tehuantepec to San Cristobal de las Casas

To Cancun, paradise of Mayan artifacts

Mayan power and pyramids

Mexico, 31 states, *Estados Unidos Mexicanos*

One hundred eleven million people

Mexico City, once the Aztec Capital, *Tenochtitlan* in the

language of *Nahuatl*

Sinking into Lake Texcoco, six inches a year

Once a hegemony created from trade and cultural exchange

Marriages and families

Art and language

Agriculture and poetry

Until the conquering Aztec came

Came and asked for tribute

Tlacaelel burned the ancient books as lies to write his own

Burned books as sacrifices to new gods

Young men played lethal games

The loser of the game *Tiachtl*

Sacrificed that the sun might move

That his blood might nurture wars

Wars called Flower Wars

Wars to conquer families

To make irrigation systems

And beautiful gardens

Gardens of flowers

The Spanish came on horses

Bringing small pox and typhus

Gardens of disease

Gardens of destruction

Wiping out entire populations

While Mayans and Incas

Farther south

Built great pyramids and cities

Until the dryness of the earth

Conquered and destroyed their life

Destroyed their flowers

Today the earth warms

And cities sink

The flowers of Mexico

Are trampled underfoot

By wars inspired by gardens

Shot by guns inspired by gardens

Marijuana, heroin gardens

Corporate gardens

Opium gardens

Lovely poppies

Latifundios

Demand tribute

Human tribute

Children's tribute

Human coyotes howl in greed

Killing the recalcitrant

With weapons from their northern neighbors

Herding lambs to flowerless tracts

Flowerless tracts of desert land

Flowerless gardens

Where Immigration and Customs Enforcement

Rake the flowerless soil

Of all human traces

Where organized crime pollutes the struggling vegetation

 Monsanto strangles *minifundios* corn

The peasants' last resource in Mexico

Land of gardens

Expelled from their own gardens

Seeking refuge ever northward

There too they find no surcease in the U.S. no relief

So the tide now folds back southward

Despairing people pushed back southward

Like a glacier of intolerance

The tide now flows again towards Mexico

Now again flows back towards Mexico

The lambs have turned

Have turned again to look for flowers

Dawn in San Francisco

Dawn in San Francisco

Transparent sky

Lit with blues, whites, grays

Populated with gulls, parrots, pigeons

Migrating birds of myriad species

Seemingly oblivious to

Climate change

Dying bees

Neonicotinoids

Ubiquitous carcinogens

Contrails betraying weather manipulation

Acidifying oceans

Three mile wide gyros of plastic

Churning in the seas

Mountains of landfill

Spilling into rivers

And children's playgrounds

Land fractured by oil companies

Encouraging earthquakes

Seemingly oblivious to

Asbestos and carbon particulates

Sweeping through the streets

Of the poor

As buildings evolve

Over destroyed

Lead-leaking

Old homes

Of the poor

To regenerate neighborhoods

Of the poor

To take those neighborhoods

From the poor

For those

Who can afford

Clean new buildings

Built on the backs

Of the poor

Built by the backs

Of the poor

Waking to the

Dawn in San Francisco

Transparent sky

Limpid horizon

Sweet cold breeze

Beautifully indifferent

To the world

It greets each morning

Departing Phoenix

Departing Phoenix airport
Clusters of homes
Dilute gradually into lines and cracks
Highways and green lines
Suggesting meadows
Sliced with urbanity
Become more like mold
Insinuating itself
Into cracks of a giant hand
Now mountains rise
Pushing up through green grey shadows
Foothills become square plots
Of courageous or misled agriculturalists
Subsiding quietly into plains and pustules
Flattened cones
Desolate to the human brain
Yet home to tortoises
Snakes spiders
Burrowing creatures
Hardy plants slide into
Sketches of an approaching city
Spots of human industry
Density
Intimacy
Hospitals families malls coffee shops
Dogs cats small birds
Clutch at sparse trees and scraggly vegetation
Thrusting from a desert mottled with fringed blushes
Curling into bumping hills and valleys
Folding unfolding pleating trailing dust

Attempting to paint itself again
Green upon grey plains
Sliced by the intrepid Interstate Highway
Subsiding into rugged dry cracks
Of parched and broken earth
A lake bounds out suddenly boldly
Then disappears into flatland
Hundreds of patches at the ends of dirt roads
Auger an enormous chemical marsh
Viscous green chemical blue
Spreads out screaming at the land
Enormous orange squares
Float grey white liquid
While flag-shaped plots of despair
Mark the ends of roads
Thousands of grey dry flags
Green center pivot claims a space
From my high perch what seems desolate
May reveal beauty viewed closer
My eye is like that of a giant
Who sees little in the scale of things
The eye of a spider views a garden
In a speck of parsley
A wonderland in a seed
I am too far to see beauty in the
Dry flag patches of a grey yellow earth
A tiny aircraft hovers beneath
Like a dragonfly
Then disappears

The Waxen Moon

The moon is waxen

Pale behind her veil

Allowing her face to show

Only briefly

In the humid skies

Shyness becomes the moon

When her face is full

Her features

Wax indistinct

Mouth

Muted tones

Murmuring

Softly

Behind

Silken

Screens

The Moon Behind Digital Clouds

The moon

Behind dark

Digital clouds

Performs a dance

Drawing her open

Fingers

Across

Demure

Lunacy

While

Starry attendants

Carry her veil

Through eons

Of time

Swirling about her

As dervishes

In slow

Motion

Through

Uncharted

Space

Cedar and the Wind

Cedar owe allegiance to the wind

Blowing gusts flatten

Fragrant boughs of evergreen

Creating limbs of grace

Above gnarled trunks

Anemoi dance

Swinging among branches

Rolling along needles

Bouncing on

Fat and flattened

Hands

Reaching upward

Palms

Shrugging

In surrender

To their sculptor

Anemoi

Anemoi

Anemoi

The wind

Last Blush

Telegraph Hill is bathed in light

Peach houses climb her slopes

Leaning over green trees

Filled with sleepy birds

Nestling into a North beach night

A single gull swoops

Like a lone sentinel

Bidding goodbye

To the last light

Of day

White clouds

Turn grey

Then blush

Pink

And slide

Into pale

Invisibility

Evening Cradles

Coit Tower

Stands sentinel

Over its domain

Of pale stucco houses

Climbing down sloping hills

Telephone poles

March upward

Cables stretched across

Corners and intersections

Deserted by their bird choirs

Now silent

Nestling beneath the cables

In leafy

Treetop

Cradles

Right to Food

The right to food
Is a fundamental human right
 Fundamental to life
Like breath
Or sleep
Fundamental to life
Like love
And learning
Freedom
And happiness
The right to food
Implies the right of food
To be pure
Unadulterated
Free of manipulation
For profit
Implies the right of food
To be itself
An apple to remain an apple
A rose to remain a rose
For by any other name
Or genome modification
It might not smell as sweet
Nor reproduce heirloom children
Inheritors of its ancestral uniqueness

My Hyphen

I lie on a hyphen

Joining my birth name

And the name of my late husband

Two worlds joined by a hyphen

I climb around my hyphen

Looking at my Swedish heritage

And back at my Chinese Hawaiian love

My hyphen mixes me up

Into pieces of the world

Once my hyphen joined me to my children's father

Joined me to other pieces of DNA

A piece that gave my daughter a tiny bit of sub-Saharan

Which she says makes her music better

And lots of Italian pieces for my son and daughter

Who grew up in Germany speaking German and English

Learning a little Turkish and French

Discovering as adults their Italian DNA

Pieces of the world shared by other pieces

All mixed up

I swing from my hyphen

Do push-ups and summersaults

And finally sit like a Buddha

To meditate on my hyphen

September Dolphin Hunt

In Taiji on Monday September 1
Dolphins will be herded into a cove
For capture or slaughter
Tradition demands that this continue
Although Mercury levels in dolphin
Are too high for safe human consumption
Attempts to add them to school lunches
Brought criticism and was discontinued
Deaths in Taiji whose people consume dolphins year round
Are 50% higher than other villages
Global condemnation of the September dolphin drive
Continues as does the hunt
Pipes are hit with sticks around the cove to frighten dolphins
To interrupt their exquisite sonar systems
Causing them in terror to swim into the cove
Where they are prisoners until the hunt begins
Again this year the marine mammals will be hunted
And caught along with orcas and porpoises
If they are unlucky enough to be caught
In a cove in Taiji this September
Where gentle dolphins find their way into human inhumanity
While so many of their brothers and sisters
Have already succumbed to an oil spill in Mauritius
Due to human negligence evoking protest
While dolphins die

Chalk

Small town America
Saleh in Washington
Draws "Black Lives Matter"
On their sidewalks in chalk
Cited for nuisance
Cited for graffiti
By the town authorities
Sprayed as they sit on their artwork
Sprayed as the city sprays away the chalk
Neighbors come out
And invite them to draw on their sidewalks
Even the military veteran says
We need to wake up
Our community needs to support black lives
And Hispanic lives
As we have failed to do in our schools
And in this community
Offenses for chalk drawings have seen their day in court
Charges dismissed
We in Saleh must embrace our community
White, black, brown
We must draw in chalk
Our support of Black Lives Matter

The Sky is Old

The sky is old
Wisps of grey cover her ears
Wrinkles deepen in old clouds
As they float upon the evening
Covering her wise face
Her veil is embroidered with silver
The Milky Way flung over her shoulder
Seductively
Occasionally one hears her grumbling
While her eyes still sparkle with lightning
In summer storms
And sometimes one hears the creek of her bed
As she settles to sleep in craggy mountains
With her partner the moon
Or wakes to greet the sun
While birds remove her nightshirt
That covered her blue beauty at night
Bathing her face with morning mist
Refreshing her make-up
Blue on blue
Cloud on cloud

After the Holidays

The world stretches

Yawns

Regrets

Holiday decorations

Wilt

While rain

Beats at the window

My umbrella sags in the doorway

Wet boots lie before the heater

The rain pours suddenly

Out of the sky

As if I had just unzipped

The pocket of a cloud

Now night has left streets wet

While rain has blown away

Into dark sky

Leaving the air cold and humid

Staring at empty stockings

On New Year's Day I raced with others

Into the surf of Ocean Beach

But first I visited his bench

And looked out to the ocean

Where my love would want to be

And where I might find him

Again

Fog

The fog ate up the city
Vestiges of thought remained
Clinging to her teeth
A bird knocked at my window
Slipping into nothingness
The fog smothered the city
In feathers
Spilling from a pillow of light
Gulls flew through feathers
Unaware of their kinship
The fog walked silently
Holding hands with ghosts
Disappearing in the morning air
To sounds of bells
Smoke rises
Reaching up into the afternoon fog blanket
Dissipating in the brilliant sun
Hiding herself not so discretely
Above a fog-drenched city

My Shadows

I walked in the night

On a cold sidewalk

Under streetlights

Seeing my shadow lengthen

As I walked

The light gave me a second shadow

Within the first

And then a third

I looked over my shoulder

To see where the shadows ended

Knowing they would be hiding

As I walked away from the light

My shadows disappeared

I imagined them

Dancing

Somewhere

Under the sidewalk

Moon Sketch

The moon was just a sketch
Someone had begun to trace
A partial circle
And stopped
Cutting
Into the darkness

The First Rose

We sing of the last rose of summer
But it is the first rose that we remember
The delicate first bud
That first tentative blossom
Holding on for dear life
Alone on its bush
Unaware
That she
Is the
Promise

Doors of Janus

Janus slides out of December

And falls through her door

Into a new year

Plunging pell- mell

Into January

While the door

Locks behind her

And winter

Hides

The key

Raindrops over cities

Raindrops circumnavigate foggy cities

Looking for a way inside

Cutting a window in clouds

To peer through

Finally wringing themselves out

Exhausted

On a rag of sky

Rain Continues

Rain continues
Obliquely insistent
Yet hesitantly apologetic
Knowing her slanted siege
Was unexpected
To all who welcomed
Her clear blue morning skies

Tone Shadows

He plays guitar
Under the light
Fingers create
Dappling shadows
Over strings
Plucked sounds
Dance about the room
Sound shadows
Raining soft echos
On the shaft of the guitar

Roads from Al-Mutanabbi Street, Baghdad, Iraq

All roads lead from Al-Mutanabbi Street

Built from poetry

Built on roads now desolate with destruction

Now bearing witness to the aftermath

Of terror and death

Yet still holding the name of a poet

The poet Mutanabbi

Born almost a thousand years

After Jesus had walked the streets of Nazareth

And was crucified for questioning

Killed for making friends with outcasts

The poet Mutanabbi claimed

Horses, night, and the desert as his friends

And the sword, the spear, paper, and the pen

Twenty six ghosts walk Al- Mutanabbi Street

Ghosts who brush by the old open air market

Market of books

Market of ideas

Market of Mutanabbi

Bombed on March 5, 2007

By a suicide bomber and a car

Killing over two dozen souls

Injuring over one hundred more

Where the books still talk among themselves

Sneeze at their own dust

Remember their ancient stories

And the terrifying day of their demise

Ghosts of books spilling out into the street

Where children play

In the rubble of literacy

Not to be forgotten

All streets lead to Al-Mutanabbi Street

All streets lead from Al-Mutanabbi Street

The cobbles watch the poets

Remember the horses and wagons

Remember the children

The cobbles talk among themselves

Of live poets

And dying remnants

Ripped from an open market

Twelve years ago

All streets of the oppressed

All streets where poets and artists dwell

Are today Al-Mutanabbi

Are today the books and ideas

Talking among themselves

Of live poets and dying remnants

Whose blood will glow through history

In every city

In every street

Where books may bleed

The Child and the Sky

The child ran to the sky
Asking for blue ribbons
To tie up a flower she found
Floating in the Rio Grande
A child ran to the sky
Asking for blue
Asking for her mother
To give her a flower
Tied in blue

A Child and Doors

A child looked out on blue
And drew a door upon blue sky
Opening the door to see her mother
Yet finding only another door
Opening into another door
Doors upon doors
Opening on paths of blue
And a child's footsteps
Walking on blue
Through countless doors
Searching for her mother

The child and the Tree

The child climbed a tree
All the way to the top
Resting as she climbed
On swaying limbs
She viewed a vast expanse
Spread out below
And felt the wind
Rushing through the branches
Talking to the trees
Talking to the leaves
Singing story

The Child and the Star

The child rests upon a star
Bright and luminous
Floating through space
Floating through time
Beyond light and air
Beyond dreams
Singing into never
Resting upon ever
Waiting for her star
To carry her
Home

We Walked along the River

We walked along the river
Hand touching hand
Only sensing touch
In spring sunlight
Walking by the river
Hearing nothing
But the sound of sun
And light of touch
The depth of air
The song of silence

I followed Your Path

I followed you along the path
Looking for mushrooms
Smelling earth
Almost hearing fungi growing
In magic circles
Under forest trees
And damp leaves
I followed you
Wanting only to follow your path
Your broad back
To fit my feet into the imprints
Of your shoes

Slavery in the Name of Jesus

Over three hundred years ago
Slaves were brought from Africa
Victims of politics, injustice and yes,
Christianity
The first slave ship was named Jesus
Jesus of Lubeck
Commandeered by John Hawkins
Owned by Queen Elizabeth
First sending Africans to the Caribbean
To work for white masters
If they survived the journey
The ships returned
With rum, sugar, textiles and tea
To enrich the British Empire
Later America did the same
Transporting black Africans
In cramped, diseased lower decks
To serve plantation owners
If they survived the journey
And make them wealthy
Returning the ships full of cotton
Goods for African traders
Goods to create wealth
On the backs of blacks
 Sir John Newton
Composer of the hymn
"Amazing Grace"
As well as "How Sweet the Name of Jesus sounds"
Sent slaves to America
Sanctifying slavery
With words of the apostle Paul
Exhorting slaves to be submissive

To their masters
To be submissive
To pervasive injustice
King James I
Of the King James Version of the Bible
Owned and sold slaves
Originally sent to eponymous
Jamestown
Quoting the Bible
To justify the horror
Of slavery
An institution
That made possible
Capitalism
And wealth
For the British Empire
And later
For plantation owners
In white America
America built on slavery
Lynching
Violence and murder
Built on the black African
The first pillar
Of capitalism
British empire
And American empire
Built on slavery
Built on injustice
Built on greed
Built on man's inhumanity to man
Planted with evil
Reaping still the fruits of that evil
Evil brought here once on a ship named Jesus

A waning Moon

The moon was waning
As I am waning
Wondering if I will become just a sliver
And then disappear
Or perhaps an angel will find my silver hammock
And rock herself into an idea of me
Or the moon

Sea Art

We find wood upon the beach
Smoothly molded into pieces of sculpture
Fashioned by the ocean
The tides, sand and shore
Artwork left by the sea
We find sand dollars
Some perfectly shaped
Others broken
Dollars of the sea
Never meant to exploit or bribe
Seldom traded
Saved by grandchildren
Delicate designs on the sandy dollar surface
Examined and caressed like sand itself
Artwork of the sea

Cat and the Moon

I imagine the moon
As if it were a ball
Chased by a witch's cat
Followed by shadows of clouds
Curling like cat's tails
Pursuing the moon
Although I know
That is perfectly absurd
I still imagine it
And think what fun
If the cat were to take
The witch's broom
To play croquet
With the moon
Hitting it through hoops
Made of stardust

Hidden in Humor

The grass is green
Upon the scene
Of Shakespeare's folly
Jolly Falstaff
Never lean
Had sooner been
An amorous knight
Of fulsome sight
Though Mrs. Ford
Would feign impose
Her own humiliations
Yet all goes well
From hill to dell
So long the audience roars
While underneath the lyric cadence
Never dull a newfound radiance
Humor hides yet must disclose
The genius of Sir William's prose

Prayer is Intuitive

Prayer is intuitive
We know monkeys in West Africa
Climb to the tops of trees
To welcome the dawn
All animals can be silent
In the peace of nature
My son as a baby would crawl
To a special spot in the road
Next to our cottage in France
To watch the sunset
The boulders in great valleys
Radiate glory from the sun
As the lakes and oceans
Reflect back a golden road
The sun walks in farewell
Saying prayers to the day

A Single Sparrow Meditates

A single sparrow meditates
Upon the cable crossing my street
The cable seems made for her
Perhaps for sparrow yoga
Maybe even pigeon yoga too
Tolerance is in the air

A single sparrow comes to munch
At my birdfeeder on the balcony
She tries each side
Each window
I go out to fill it with seed
Although it is raining
And I and my bare feet get wet

A single sparrow flies to my window
Perching on the grate
Fluffing her wings
Drying off a bit
Under the eaves
Then flies off again
Into the light rain

At the coffee shop
I look outside
And see a single sparrow
Drinking from a puddle
Full of fresh rainwater
While raindrops
Continue to splash

Variable

The sky is variable

As music is variable

Tones thoughts impulses

Snowflakes animals' hooves

Fingernails clumps of yarn

Nothing is the same

Ever anywhere

Yet sometimes

One can stretch

The inevitably variable

Into exquisite expression

A Bach fugue

Perfect

Yet stretched shaded

Just so

Spontaneous

Almost unknowable

As humanity

Reaches into the fugue

Molds transformation

Squeezes passion out

In tiny drops

Upon the variable

Air

No Choice

Rain here
Sunshine in Tijuana
Or across the border
In California
Not that it matters
Children still have fevers
In unheated cages
Trading in one suffering
For another
Marching from violence
From poor countries
Whose corruption
Catalyzed by US meddling
Has led to unemployment
And meager food supplies
Marching into another country
Whose wealth at the top
Leads to another kind of corruption
And violence
Upon the poorest of the poor
Those who seek asylum
Because they have no choice
Because they have no voice

In Kiruna

In Kiruna
In Sweden
A country where my ancestors lived
In Kiruna
Ninety miles north
Of the Arctic Circle
The city is moving
Ghosts cry from eons beneath the city
Ghosts cry from the mine
Over a mile beneath
Over two miles long
Still rich in iron ore
And crumbling
As the surface of the city
Subsides
The deer gaze
Glassy eyed
While ice breaks under their feet
Collecting in chunks
Like dice thrown
From wary ghosts
Of ancient times
The Sami mourn
Vestiges of their land
Sacrificed to an underground mine
The people mourn their city
Mourn the loss of valley and mountains
As they move to windy flatlands
And the mine continues
To kill with silicosis
And satisfy those who exploit the land
For temporal wealth

While the reindeer move quietly
Large eyes wondering
Gazing at the dancing Northern Lights
Who sing of moon and sun
And help to weave
The Milky Way
Illuminating runes
Telling story

Kiruna

Poles of lights

Dance

Snow blows

Particles hover

Over ice

Modern day igloos

Ice rooms

Frozen beds

Surrounded by

Ice sculpture

Plains of frozen river

Paced by dogs pulling sleighs

Await the dancing lights

Of midnight in

Kiruna

The Birds are Back

The birds are back
And not yet March
I forget how soon
They yearn again
To call their mates
To call the sun to wake
And ride the sky
The birds are back
And sing of rain
And sun and trees
And air and wind
And fluff themselves
Airbrush their feathers
Till they lift
And fly themselves
Away

The Fence Stands

The fence
Stands as if alive
Menacing
Or comforting
Imprisoning
Or protecting
Separates
The wall twists
Embraces
Repels
Challenges

The Bird Rests Upon Ideas

The bird rests upon ideas

Her wings closed

She is like a Buddha

Carrying the world

In her feathers

Warm and round

Relentlessly dense

Questioning

Motion thought

Direction

Solitary in thought

Becoming

Separate

Wing to eye

Split in motion

And sight

Floating in particles

Of neverness

And always

Her eyes find

Closed wings

And hide

In feathered

Silence

Early Spring

The air is alive

As seasons stretch

Their arms

Holding hands through time

The sky breathes

In autumn mists

Summer silence

Winter chill

Expecting spring

As blossoms

Burst shyly

From naked branches

Wondering

If they are

On time

Or perhaps

A little early

A Fish in the Mariana Trench

A strange fish
Swims in darkness
Plastic shrimp
Surround it
Old strands
Of straws
Wrap themselves
Around its fins
Red and white
Stripes
Float into its mouth
Sliding past its tiny bones
Into luminous cavities
Nesting resting
In place of food
In the darkness

Another Day

A small bird sings
Lighting the dawn
With her song
Calling the buds
To blossom
The insects
To rub their wings
In ecstasy
The worms to crawl
The crows to caw
In expectation
Of another day

Broken

Who gives up when your body is broken?

Angels, sitting on your shoulders

Flutter and murmur

They stare into the great void

Like a painter at his canvas

A poet at her book

Seeing emptiness and expectation

Bruised bones awaiting healing

Canvas expecting colors

Paper welcoming words

Stone expecting to be carved

Into life

Body, canvas, paper, stone

Finite elements

In the mystery of the infinite

Pouring itself into expressions

Of that which once was

Of that which is or will be

Age

Age invites discretion

Not excess

Age invites knowledge

Invites wisdom

Age is a fool's garden

Seeded with tempting flowers

Of imprudence

Dancing with honey bees

Gathering nectar

Fanned with winds blowing

Perfumes of seduction

One last chance whispers the garden

Before her flowers close

Her bees curl into the night

How much time do you have?

You may slip on the ice

You may break your body

You may lose your way

Fight your path through darkness

And frailty of age

Yet dare to venture

One more time

Before the curtain

Falls

Resting with a Broken Leg

My bed is a tangle of

Clothes

Papers

Envelopes

Unopened mail

A computer

Two phones

Work to be done

An empty coffee cup

Sits randomly by two crutches

My leg rests supinely

Almost heroically

Amid the clutter

Knowing she cannot move

Without pain

And will remain

Until another urgency

Demand

She rise again

Everness

How did chaos break into eternity

How did molecules find their way

Into the vastness of never and ever?

How did split atoms and moist air

Make a baby cry

After a dinosaur

Had left his mighty paw

Immersed in teeming lime

Not to mention time?

How did a hummingbird

Find her way into a flower

The wind crack open limbs of trees

The oceans carve great valleys

From which tiny blooms

And tinier insects

Might find their homes?

How did eternity

Allow an island of finite matter

Living growth

Stone and snails

Children with pails

Shovels and sails

Bedrock and laughter

Penetrate its

Everness?

Walking Through the Mirror

Imagine walking through the mirror

Fluttering into another dimension

Catching hold of the sky yet feeling nothing

Endless sky yet empty

Imagine walking through the mirror

As through air

Boundless

Horizonless

Moon and sun rising and setting together

Like the midnight sun above all boundaries

Constellations wrapping themselves

Around the journey through a mirror

Shining through the other side

Glimpsing nothing

Wind and hail

Blowing a trumpet voluntary

Throwing all of life into a skyless sky

All blues yet blueless

Full of yesterdays todays tomorrows

Never and always

Boundless unbounded

Lost in the music of

Silence

On the other side

Of the mirror

Patience

Patience is easy
As one grows older
There is no rush
No push
To cross
Another hill
Find another treasure
Swim another sea
There is no need
To win
No need
To lose
And yet one forgets
Not to struggle
One forgets
To rest
In the restless cradle
Of our world
Whose horizon
Still beckons
With a new sunrise
Each golden
Morning

Easter

Everything heals

Broken bones

Knit together

Again and again

The cut closes

Sodden leaves of autumn

Dig into the moist earth

Where new green shoots

Push tender faces

Up towards light

Everything renews

Even stones

Roll themselves away

From sepulchers of earth

That life may resurrect itself

Within each soul

Assange Sanctuary Violated

Assange
Arrested
For free speech
Free press
A danger to
The US war efforts
Opening up Pandora's box
On US war crimes
Secrets that should not be secret
Tearing off the curtain
Hiding our country's crimes
In Afghanistan, Iraq, Yemen
Videos of Americans
Killing civilians and journalists
Records of war crimes
Discovered by Chelsea Manning
Also imprisoned
For disclosing hidden truths
Assange
Sought by our government
Found sanctuary in London
In the Ecuadorian Embassy
Today his Sanctuary was violated
After nearly seven years
We remember
Fifty years ago
Daniel Ellsberg
Surrendered to arrest
In Boston
June, 1971
For copying the Pentagon Papers
Without security clearance

For giving the New York Times
What they subsequently published
Yet Ellsberg was vindicated
When Nixon's plumbers were discovered
To have vandalized his psychiatrist's office
Criminal acts to subvert knowledge
Of criminal acts
To subvert truth
The public
Should know
Of our crimes
Against the Vietnamese
To subvert truth
Of our war crimes
Our crimes against humanity
Just as again
Assange and Manning
Refused to keep secret
What the public
Should know
Of our crimes
In Afghanistan
Of our crimes
In Iraq
Of our crimes
Against humanity
Our war crimes
In the hope that divulgence of truth
Might bring an end
to further war and suffering
Might bring an end to lies
Might bring a springtime of hope
Might bring a birth of honesty and honor
To our nation and our world

Wrinkles

Wrinkles on my hand
Heaving hills cross space
Like hills of earth
Wrinkles of earth
Traversing her history
Her evolution of change
Earthquakes
Water
Hurricanes
Fire
Conspire to form
Rivulets of change
Massive mountains
Valleys
A giant's wrist
A giant's hand
Aged through the years
Into rivers and valleys
We ourselves
May view
Or traverse
Hike to their summits
To view sunset or sunrise
Over rivulets
Of earth's own wrinkles

I am the Wounds

I am Gaza Afghanistan Iraq Yemen

I am countries ravaged by war

Inflicted with wounds

By the US or its allies

Israel Saudi Arabia

I am a mother

I am a child

I am a refugee

From war Made in the USA

I look to justice in international courts

Or the United Nations

Whose charter

Signed by the USA

Demands human rights

Underlined by its

Declaration on Human Rights

Which floats blankly

With other UN documents

Arrogantly unsigned

By our congress

I look for hope

I look for peace

And only see those

Who seek justice

Repudiated by the USA

Warrior for the last vestiges

Of colonialism

I see visas rejected

By those who would hold

The USA responsible

For its war crimes

Would hold Israel responsible

For its war crimes

I am Gaza

I am Yemen

I am Afghanistan

I am Iraq

I am a mother

I am a child

I am a refugee

From injustice made in the USA

And see no redress in the courts of law

No hope under the feet

Of Mother Liberty

I only ask

Where can I find

Humanity?

Where can I

Take the pulse of a heart

That beats

For me?

Kidnap and Murder of Palestinians

Palestinians are kidnapped each day by Zionist Israelis
55,000 Palestinians behind Israeli bars since 1948
Even after the Deir Yassim massacre of Palestinians
Of Palestinians protecting the gates to their homes
Tortured, humiliated, abused
Shinbet wreaks its vengeance
Assuages its guilt for massacre upon massacre
Injustice upon injustice
Gaza, West Bank, Occupied Lebanon
Sabra and Shatila
Refugee camps of Palestinians in Lebanon
Scenes of rape, murder
Atrocity upon atrocity by Christians by Zionists
Babies ripped from wombs
Toddlers decapitated
Scenes of horror are reported
Women left dead with legs apart
Ripped skirts high and bloody in 1982
The years pass as USA remains complicit in horror
Complicit in Zionist atrocities
Israeli rape and murder of Palestinians remains unredeemed
We pray for the glimmer of a glowworm of hope
That peace someday might light the skies of Palestine

Photo of names of 107 victims of Deir Yassim Massacre

243

Carrot

I remember a small carrot

In my Aunt's garden

I had never pulled a carrot up

From a garden

I remember the smell of earth

And carrot

And the feel of the stem of the carrot

In my hand

I was seven

Or maybe less

I sat with that carrot

And smelled earth

And when I took a bite

I felt

I was eating

The world

Or rather

I felt

The world

Had absorbed me

In the smell and taste

Of a carrot

I became earth and carrot

Carrot and earth

A Slice of Moon

Last week I saw the moon

Or rather

Exactly half of the moon

Like a slice of lemon

Perfectly sliced

In half

Bright yellow

Like a slice of lemon

Stamped against the sky

No stars

No wisps of cloud

No fog

Or rain

Or wind

Just a slice of lemon

Too big for me to eat

Glowing brightly

Against the sky

Coral An Animal

Since coral is an animal
It belongs in my menagerie
Along with the ducks and turtles
And yet coral is not just an animal
It is a nursery where animals can be safe
Little fish
Turtles
Baby eels
All can hide in their coral reef
While it slowly grows
Chambers and coves for its brood
While it slowly turns to sand
Through its digestion by parrot fish
And humuhumunukunukuapua'a
And becomes nesting ground for sea anemone
For crabs and clams
While it maintains a habitat
Essential to the life of our ocean and its marine animals
Especially its babies
Even the babies of sharks
The coral reef asks only that we temper our carbon emissions
So that it may not suffocate
Or fail to provide clean water for its animal friends
That its beautiful waters may not grow acid with pollutants
That it may live and grow
And help save our planet
Its waters and all its marine life
As an animal
Coral asks only
That it be treated
With dignity

What Happened to the Hummingbirds?

What happened to the hummingbirds?
The air is silent
The wind still
I hear a chirp somewhere
Far away
The eaves of my houses seem vacant
What happened to the hummingbirds?

What happened to the squirrels?
I used to see them
Scampering about the park
Today they are absent
Are they hiding from the dogs
Or from the hawks?
What happened to the squirrels?

What happened to the sparrows?
They used to peck away
Beneath the tables
Outside the coffee house
Or scramble under the trees in the park
Today they are absent
What happened to the sparrows?

Perhaps it is just a silent moment
When hummingbirds
Squirrels
Sparrows
Are busy
In their own world
And yet
I miss them

I miss seeing the homeless
Normally sitting on the corner
With bags and blankets
I worry that they were taken away
Locked up somewhere
Maybe they found homes
But I can't be sure
I miss seeing them
Because I worry
Why they are not there
I miss them

I miss my darling
Yesterday I grilled on the roof
And waited for him to come
And join me
Knowing he was gone
But worrying about him
Wondering where he went
Wondering if there is a better place
If he is flying in the sky
Or swimming in the ocean
Many dimensions away
Perhaps he is busy
In his own new world
And yet
I miss him

Square and Peg Conundrum

Compatibility or collaboration

Synergy or empathy

Peg in peg

Square in square

Or peg in square

Or square in peg

Reuleaux or Toeplitz

Corners in which to dream

Corners in which to collaborate

Extra spaces

Nooks and crevices

Unnamed areas to hide

Edges of infinity

To remember

To forget

To disappear

Or to find harmony

Discover the glue

That joins the universe

Cube in Circle

Castle in Pond
Enjoys her solitary seat
Her ponderous perch
Views segments underneath
Chord and arc
One on each side
Room for ducks to swim
And clamber over their arc
To another arc
Around the corner
To visit other ducks
Or perhaps a swan
Four arcs to discover
Before returning to the first
And gaze up to the castle
An impenetrable chord
An edge of concrete
The edge of her first segment
As the edge of each segment
Geometrically a chord
Four chords completing each segment
Congruence in harmony
A circle where ducks can dream
And moss can grow
And Pythagoras can sit and play his lyre
Listen to four hammers swung by a blacksmith
Creating musical chords
Then pluck the strings of his lyre in musical scales
Harmony and phrase
Arc and chord
Accompanying the splash of ducks
Sliding from segment to segment

Where is Tomorrow?

Where is tomorrow
When yesterday is lost
Will tomorrow be adopted for a while
Until she too is lost in somewhere else
An orphan between now and then
Can we return to time once spent
On milk nickels in a childhood long past
Where pickles too cost nickels
Someone's dad gave his little boy to buy
When he bought instead some chewing gum
Or something else that has disappeared
In the fissures of time and childhood
Chalk on the sidewalk for hopscotch
Pony rides in the park
Walking to school unsupervised
Safe in the sunshine of a city
Now lost like Brigadoon
In mists of childhood
Never to return with
Weenie roasts on a beach
Clams dug up with a young dad in a hat
Eaten with ketchup on the kitchen table
Pictures of a past now faded
Smiling from ragged edges of time
Some stuck on a refrigerator
Some slid behind other memories
Some just hiding at the bottom
Of a rabbit hole
Waiting for a different Alice
To bring them back to life
In someone's imagination

Little Girl and China

Brilliant sun out my window

This side of the world

I was told as a little girl

If I dug far enough

I would reach China on the other side

I tried to dig to China

Digging with my shovel on the beach

But it seemed like a lot of work

I knew the same brilliant sun

Shone in China

When here it was night

And people were there

But spoke a different language

And maybe they saw different stars

I wondered if someone from China

Would crawl out of a hole

If sometime someone

Who dug far enough

To get to the other side of the earth

Would see our brilliant sun

Or maybe the big dipper

In the night sky

When they crawled out

Of the hole they dug from China

And smile at me

A Tiny Flying Thing

A tiny fly or flea
Bounces around my window
And my bed
He had an adventure earlier
When I tried to crush him
On the window
He's still flying
So I'll just revel with him
In being alive

Silken Fog

A lady's silk scarf curls
Around my favorite ferns
While chipmunks tease
Seeming to pull the scarf with them
Up their neighboring pine
And silken fringes shudder with the wind
While fingernails of pinecones
Scratch moist earth
Succumbing to soft caresses
From a vagrant fog

Colors

There are more blues and greens
Than anyone could number
More shades of pink
I see in cheeks of baby's slumber
More reds in velvet, silk and sunrise
Golds in tones of autumn
Muddy shoes stomping in ponds
Swirling browns upon the bottom
A universe of colors
Painting every brand new dawn
Forever bursting from my garden
Dandelions upon the lawn
I think if I were still a child
I'd climb the tallest tree
And count out loud below me
All the colors I could see

Touch

Touch
Hand on cheek
Lips caressing
Soft skin
Arms become like silken scarves
Or angel feathers
Hands find secret spaces
Touching warmth
Legs thighs
Mystery lies
Between small places
Dark and yielding
He said I caress
As if I were his body
Perhaps two bodies
Are as one
In touch

Inequity and Infrastructure

Twenty-six people hold half the wealth of the whole world

And people still are starving

Still are floating on matchbox boats and plastic rafts

To escape starvation or violence or war

Another baby washed on shore in Kos

Like Alan Kurdi washed up drowned in Turkey five years ago

Every day families die with babies and children

Crossing from Iraq or Syria to Greece

I waited with mothers in Kos

With eight new babies

Waiting for a boat to Athens

They could no longer stay in tents in Kos

There was no sanitation no food no water

For their babies

Most of the world is scrambling for life

Most of the world needs health care

Most of the world needs

What less than one percent could give

To help create an infrastructure

On which the rest might build their lives

First Citizen (from Coriolanus, Shakespeare)

We are accounted poor citizens, the patricians good. What authority surfeits on would relieve us: if they would yield us but the superfluity, while it were wholesome, we might guess they relieved us humanely; but they think we are too dear: the leanness that afflicts us, the object of our misery, is as an inventory to particularise their abundance; our sufferance is a gain to them Let us revenge this with our pikes, ere we become rakes: for the gods know I speak this in hunger for bread, not in thirst for revenge.

Birds and Home

A bird flies away to die
Flies away to find a nest
To rest until its time has come
To fly back into nature
All things find their way
Back into the spirit world
Back into the clouds
Birds and angels
Wait silently
In nests woven long ago
To welcome us
Home

A Star

Look at a star
Thinking it alone in the vast universe
Unaware that it is seen by you
And countless others
Unaware of its innumerable neighbors
In the skies about it
It is merely there
And all the world and far beyond
In which our spirit dwells
Visible and invisible
Seen and unseen
Part of a vast idea
A vast thought
In a mind that is
Forever stardust

All is Beautiful

I passed a woman in the street
Beautifully dressed
Scarves and earrings
A red hat framing her face
Her dark hair fastened upwards
She looked at me and said
You are beautiful
And went her way
Like a spirit of affirmation
In a world of indifference
She walks through the streets
With her smile and stature
Her African heritage beating
And singing and laughing
And affirming this world
Embracing all
That is beautiful
And all is beautiful

Stardust

All of us are made of stardust
Science tells us
We are a pastiche of eternities
Matter flung together
In a paroxysm of creation
Dough kneaded in a garden
Full of unnamed flowers
From seeds thrown by nameless birds
And angels fluttering through clouds
Of damp and pregnant
Stardust

Fog Caresses the City

Fog caresses the city
With a damp palm
Pulling eider down over her streets
Curling into alleyways
The city shivers
Birds are silent
Seeking shelter in the eaves
From a cool foggy night

Dreams of Stardust

The birds build nests
Of fragments of stardust
And illusions
Sand from the sea
Crystals from the mountains
Bits of music from the wind and rain
And soft new green leaves
And when they have nested
And are warming their little ones
They repair the nest
With more fragments and illusions
So their little ones may dream
Of flying on stardust
While the wind rocks their nest
And when the tiny ones have fledged
And have sung their first song
Threaded with notes of dreams
The birds hear the melody of their tiny ones
Know it is their own
And fly with them
On dreams of stardust
And illusions

My Book

My book is open

Random thoughts enter its pages

Dreams of stories not yet imagined

Yet hung on ideas spun by fairies

With magic clothespins

On a line of silver held up by the stars

My book is open

Waiting for a child to smell its rapture

Hold its thoughts in open hands

Play hopscotch with the numbers

On its pages

And wish secret wishes

Held up by the stars

Connections

We are ineffably interconnected

Your words echo twice around the world

While the flutter of a butterfly's wings

Launches currents lost in space

Yet soaring to the farthermost

Ends and beginnings of our universe

Neither good nor evil inters within our bones

Yet finds itself in filaments

Woven into carpets

Carrying us with Toto into Oz

Or some unknown fairyland

Where dreams come true

Or clouds demand we wrap them

Around fragments of ideas

Awaiting judgment

Good and evil

Love and hate

Inextricable from history

Yet wound up in our destiny

Ribbons tying us together

Flowing through us back into the

Unknown oceans of our social conscience

Where fluttering butterfly wings

Dance in mists of surging waves

And move the very mountains with their power

Loyalty

Loyalty I think is to be present
To pay attention
To be aware of details and nuances
Shadows and light
Stitches through time
Stitches that connect
Loyalty listens to the story
Bonds with the idea
Remains vulnerable to another pain
Loyalty allows hurt to enter
Asks the questions that hide
Within other questions
Sees without judgment
Listens without bias
Reaches with the heart
To hear the beating of another
Loyalty is the greatest gift
Loyalty to all we love
Watering flowers and plants
Feeding birds and animals
Taking care of each other
Reaching out to help
Reaching back to protect
Seeing those you love
As their best selves
Finding good in small gestures
Touching to heal
Being there for another
Knowing the other is there too
Perhaps for you

My Friends

The lemon tree in my garden
Is unique because she is mine
I water her and admire her
She is my friend
The cloud in the sky is mine
Because I see its shape
And dream myself in its embrace
It is my friend
The sunset is mine
Because I see its colors
I fly with it
Past the horizon
It is my friend
The birds are mine
Because I want them free
And see them fly
I give them water and seed
And listen to their song
They are my friends

Together

She looked at him
And he was strong
And beautiful to her
Insecurities fled
Confidence emerged
Her look made him feel
He could do anything
The birds fly in pairs
I wonder if they make each other
Strong and beautiful
Simply by looking at each other
Ruffling each other's feathers
Following each other
Without question
Knowing together
They can do anything
Beluga whales
Seek each other out
Over a vast ocean
Stay with each other over years
Together they can go anywhere
Trees talk together
Help each other
One to one to one
In a web of mycelium
Roots and fungi
Together they weather the world
Together they are beautiful
Together they are strong
Together they are more than two
As one

Freedom and Sticks

The white crowned sparrow
Modest
With a thrilling song
Perches near my window
While another bird
Nestles in the eaves above
The birds are so sure of who they are
Their flight
Their song
Their nest
The baby blue herons flap their wings
Ready to leave their nurseries
Yet ambivalent
While their parents stand guard
Waiting for their flight
The nests seem smaller
As our own world collapses around us
When we take flight
And is changed when we return
Our nests are now tangled
Microscopic eyes sewn into foliage
Remain observing
When our nest collapses
Reeds and willows sway and fall
With the wind
A heron carries a stick in his beak
To repair the nest of his offspring
But does not fear eyes peering
As he returns to the sky
While in our own collapsing nests
Our refuge in times of pandemic
And our prison

The sticks we carry
Assure we remain guarded
Offer no connection, no protection
As we take flight
Into a sky of eyes
That cannot be escaped
Nor changed
Unless we change the world
Into which we were born
In which we once felt free
To seek our destiny
In which we once felt safe
Sheltering in place
But now demands we turn
And learn to fly again
To leave our nest in tatters
To face a world of shatters
Of questions
Of surveillance
Of oblivion
Lost in smatters
Of apathy
To what matters
Spied upon
By our own cameras
Sticks we carry
Every day
Eyes that watch us
Every way

Stars Enchant

Stars enchant
Elusive geniuses of the skies
Immense yet tiny
Unfathomably fiery
Yet cool and twinkling
Single and alone
Or covering the sky
With carpets of silver

Limu from the Sea

Limu from the sea
Hawaiian gifts
Limu huluhuluwaena
Limu lipoa Limu 'ele 'ele
Seaweed from the islands
Food
Medicine
Celebration
Limu teaches us to live simply
To accept gifts from the ocean
Cut boil thrash fry spin enjoy
Thrive on the simplicity of Limu

Bread

The baguette
Staple of French life
Under your arm
Or fastened to the bicycle rack
Hot and crispy
Minus the quignon
That crusty bite of the tip of it
Warm and fresh
You bit off when you came out of the bakery
You must buy more than one loaf
Or you will be fined these days
You must shop for multiple loaves
To fight the corona virus
When you come out of the bakery
One baguette?
Non non non
At least five to freeze or seven
You must shop once a week
Not daily
A new world to the French
Freezing baguettes?
Non non non
C'est pas français!
Mais oui! Mais oui!
C'est nécessaire
Freezing bread is not French
But a life without bread cheese and wine
Is not French
We must have our bread
Surtout et partout
Nous avons besoin de notre pain

Embarassing

Such a strange word
Like embrace
But coming from
Portuguese
Meaning noose or strap
Like barricade
Or Spanish
Meaning pregnant
Embarazada
When women feeel
Strangely out of place
As their bodies change
What is it to be embarrassed?
To feel shyly out of place?
Embarrassed
Red with shame
Timid yet not to blame
A word a look
Not to belong
Unthinking
Breaking into song
Outside with everyone seeing just you
Embarrassing but true
It's you alone who dares
But really now, who cares?

Morning on the Lagoon

A long billed curlew
And a sandy dappled willet
Danced on the shore
Of a sunny lagoon
While above
Three giant white pelicans
Showed their banded wings
Flying against the wind
From blue to blue
Great white egrets
Dipped their yellow bills
Into the water
Feathers gently ruffled
By the lagoon breeze

Loujain al-Hathlou

**In 2015 Listed 3rd among 100 most powerful Arab women
PEN Freedom Award 2019 while imprisoned**

Loujain al-Hathlou

Imprisoned in Saudi Arabia

Celebrates her third birthday in prison

She has turned 31

Experiencing only imprisonment

And torture for over two years

Electrocution of the feet and beatings

Daily bread for a young woman

Given as a reward for speaking her mind

Demanding human rights in Saudi Arabia

Demanding women's rights in Saudi Arabia

The same country that sent pilots

To America to bring down the twin towers

The same country that bombs Yemen unmercifully

That same country imprisons Loujain al-Hathlou

Who campaigned successfully

For women's right to drive

For women's right to speak out

For women's rights as human rights

Awarded for her courage

Honored for speaking truth to power

Yet remains imprisoned and tortured

By a country America considers its friend and ally

The Elephant

The elephant has a mighty brain
To move him through the vast terrain
We call the land of Africa
His trunk works like our arms and fingers
Quick or with a pat that lingers
His brain supports that nimble trunk
You've seen him plod the earth or sunk
In mud in ponds of the Sahel
A place where he will always dwell
As long as we leave him intact
With tusks and skin and teeth and back
To ride if we will just be kind
And let him use his noble mind
To guide us through his native land
Without a prod or cruel hand

Mozart and Genius

Mozart claimed genius is love
Love is music
A cloud settles on my brain
Reminding me of rain and sun
Waterfalls and forests
Riverbanks and tadpoles
Looking through clouds
I see music and Mozart

Two Birds

When two birds fly in different streams
One looks back
The other dreams
One regrets that she was mad
The other simply says, too bad
Flies into another sky
Just as blue and just as high
To find another better mate
Before he fears it grows too late
To find and love and nest and coo
And laugh with someone who makes two
While one will simply stay behind
And practice how to be more kind

Love is Like That

A little wooden elephant
Sat upon a small platform with four wheels
To the wheels was attached a string
A little boy held the string
And took the wooden elephant everywhere

Sometimes a bigger person
Held the little boy's hand
While they walked together
But the little elephant was happy
Just to be pulled on the string by the little boy
They went to the zoo and saw the monkeys
And big elephants just like her or him or them

They went sometimes to get ice cream
And the little elephant was happy
Because the little boy was happy
When the day was over
The little boy pulled the little elephant
To the stairs of his house
And took the little elephant in his arms
To go up the stairs
And home

One evening the little boy
Took the elephant in his lap
And told the little elephant
To look at the sunset with him
Someday we will go together
You and I
To find out where the sun
Goes to bed

Another night the little boy
Put the elephant in his lap
And looked at the moon
He told the little elephant
Someday we will go there
You and I
We will sleep in one of those shadows
On the moon
They look soft and comfortable
And we can look at the stars

Hammock of the Heart

Truth is hearing jazz in New Orleans
Trust is visiting those who hurt
Love is entering the heart of the beast
Or the heart of the lamb
And realizing they are the same

Every quarrel is a portal to truth
Every disagreement a door to knowledge
Forgiveness is washing the sand off your feet
To walk tip toe into another's consciousness
Leaving the sand at the door

Love is the wind that blows
Through every moment in time
That pushes the weathervane full circle
While every direction every thought every idea
Spins over and through and into love

We are born thinking we are the world
Subsumed in mother in sensation in all that is
We grow to be alone, reaching back to touch
Much that has always been inside us
Yet we have forgotten

Forgetting is a spirit world
Gathering our shadows in a soft embrace
That disappears in grace
And rests beyond the fabric of forgiveness
In the hammock of the heart

Escape into Forever

We walk into the forest of the spirit
Great canopies venture beyond our thought
We float on cones pummeled by winds
That push beyond the roots of consciousness
We climb with squirrels pulled by sunshine
Beaming a green ladder into light

We climb beyond the clouds and sun
Beyond ideas of galaxies
Beyond all constellations
Our hands hold stardust gently
Dreams of ages seeming to be deep within
And yet escape into forever

Above the forest of the spirit
We ride upon the eagle's feathered wing
Becoming all we see beneath her vision
And all we see becomes the air we sing
And smell of pine mingles with jasmine
While jasmine is the very air we breathe

And air and stars and consciousness
Become our eagle's flight
As soul emerges on her wings
And we become the night

Translation into Spanish by the author

Escapar para siempre (Escape into Forever)

Entramos en el bosque del espíritu
Grandes marquesinas se aventuran
Más allá de nuestro pensamiento
Flotamos en conos aporreados por los vientos
Que empujan más allá de las raíces de la conciencia
Escalamos con ardillas tiradas por el sol
Transmitiendo una escalera verde a la luz

Subimos más allá de las nubes y el sol
Más allá de las ideas de las galaxias
Más allá de todas las constelaciones.
Nuestras manos sostienen
El polvo de estrellas suavemente
Sueños de edades que parecen estar muy dentro
 Y sin embargo escapar para siempre

Sobre el bosque del espíritu
Cabalgamos sobre el ala emplumada del águila
Convertirse en todo lo que vemos debajo de su visión
Y todo lo que vemos se convierte en el aire que cantamos
Y olor a pino mezclado con jazmín
Mientras que el jazmín es el mismo aire que respiramos

Y el aire y las estrellas y la conciencia
Se convierten en el vuelo de nuestras águilas
Nuestra alma emerge en sus alas
Y nos convertimos en la noche

Reflections

The peahen gazes at herself
In a large and shining window
Thinking she has found a friend
Wanting to walk into the window
As we all see ourselves reflected in others
And want to walk into our reflection
Reaching out for friendship with ourselves
Seeing what we want to see
Blind to what we are and are not
Embracing our shadow and our light
Reflected in another
The peahen cannot enter her reflection
Turns away
To find her peacock
Yet again deceives herself
Forgets again that all we see
In gazing at another
Is what we want to see
Reflections of ourselves
Our own perceptions
Of reality

Year 75 after Hiroshima

Year 75 after Hiroshima
End of war
Beginning of war
A nuclear bomb
Decimated 2,000 feet above Hiroshima
No big deal
Little Boy followed by
Fat Man for Nagasaki
Not as if it did the damage
Of decimation at city level
Not as if it matters that 146,000 people died and more later
That years later
Physiological and psychological
Damage remained
Not as bad as Chernobyl or Fukushima
Where 400 times as much radioactivity was generated
Not so bad
Saved American lives by ending the war
After we had strafed Tokyo
Just to be sure
Saved lives, saved America
Far from Japanese shores
By intimidating the Soviets
So America would rule
After a war won by the allies
With Soviet domination
Now we got what we wished for
And could celebrate
The beginning of a new era
Of human destruction

Enheduanna, First Poet

The first known poet
A woman
Was born to a king
Found as an infant in a reed basket
Like Moses
Raised in a garden
Nurtured by a goddess
He the baby Sargon
Beloved of Inanna
Became cupbearer to the king
And later king himself
Unifying his kingdom Akkadia
And the Sumerians he conquered
His daughter he named priestess of Sumeria
To be their link to heaven and poet
First known poet
Enheduanna who wrote her poems
And histories of the goddesses and gods
On limestone cuneiform discs
Imprinted with her words and with her image
Words of praise for Innana her beloved goddess
And hymns surviving four thousand years
Become the story of gods through the ages
Told by the stylus of the first poet
The woman Enheduanna

Fog Flour

The fog rolls in
Edges of a lump of fairy flour
Kneaded by the gods
Bits of flour flying far above
While gods press the flour
With their bare hands
Pushing it across the bay
Then lift it
Thin and transparent
To place within the bowl of the sky

Still Life in the Window

It is morning and there is a bright sun
And yet I see stars
They are merely reflections from a ceramic lamp
Yet sparkle like stars on my window
Within reflections of the lamp
Framed by my window
As bits of pear tree leaves
Sneak into the scene
A mobile still life painting
Animated by the wind

Up and Down

We know there is no up nor down
Upon our face no smile nor frown
Just constructs of our own ideas
Like time we fashion just to please
Our need to live within a frame
A template made to give a name
To all the things we do each day
To meet a friend at noon we say
Although there really is no noon
And yet there is a road the moon
Travels each day just like the sun
Moves in the universe as one
Who knows her place her sequencing
Within the multitude a thing
We human beings would like to scope
With instruments like clocks or rope
We tie in intricate design
And so invent a thing called time
Send signals with a smile or frown
And play with thoughts of up and down

Sankofa Thoughts

Look back

Raise the past to save the present

Heal the past to save the future

Hold a blossom in your heart

An orchard in your shoe

A song among the branches

In each tree

Singing of you

Llama

A llama was found in a cave in Mexico
Split twig, four legs
Maybe made for a ritual
Maybe some child found near a rock
Maybe some child played with
Some child hugged
Some child sat with by a campfire
Or took to bed in a cave in Mexico
Nearly five thousand years ago
When tools were used to make a llama
By a mommy or daddy
Maybe for a ritual
Maybe found by a child
Whose Mommy and Daddy
Knew the universal need of children to play
Children's work as important as hunting
As important as prayers
Playing and teaching toys to run and hide
Created by tools made for gathering
Gathering pieces of things
Gathering things
For toys and art
Women's work
Children's work
The beginning of civilization

Squirrel

The squirrel said to her friend

I was rude

Last season

I didn't mean to be

And it was a long time ago

But I'm sorry

I wish I had invited you into my hole

To spend the night

But I was feeling hurt

I don't know why

It was just me, chattering too much

And not hearing you

And now it's a little late

To say, I'm sorry

And hold your paw

But the friend said

It's okay

And reached out his paw

To pat the squirrel's soft tail

The Story of Two Egrets

The snowy egret with a black bill
And yellow feet
Hovers above the bay
Darting down gracefully
To catch a fish
The great egret
With yellow bill and black feet
Stands upon the rocks
Preening his plumage
The cormorant swims below
Rising up to flap
Enormous wings above the water
To dry its feathers
While the snowy egret watches
Enamored of the great egret
With a yellow bill and black feet
Wishing they were compatible
Flies down to dance about his feathers
Pirouetting on her yellow feet
Tossing her wind-brushed feathered crown
Until the great egret slips into the bay
Then rises far above
Yellow bill into the wind
Flying far, far away
And the little snowy egret
Rises on her yellow feet
The wind brushing her white feathers
In a snowy crown
Flies up and farther up
Until she and the clouds ride on the wind
In harmony with a golden sunset
And a silver moon

Bear Family

There once were two little bears
They learned to fight each other every day
As little brothers always do
They also went fishing every day together
They always fished separately at first
But they were very little bears
And sometimes it was hard catching fish
One day one bear sat down in front of two rocks
And spread his legs so the fish swam into his lap
The other bear snapped up the fish and they had a nice lunch
They did this every day until they grew into big bears
When they were big it was easy to fish alone
But they missed fishing together
So they started catching messes of fishes together again
The girl bears started taking notice
They gathered around and smiled at the bears
The bears had so much food they shared it with the girls
Soon they were hanging out together all the time
When nighttime came they found caves near the brook
And nooks to rest and play
Soon they had more little bears
Sometimes the little bears fought as little bears do
But they learned to work together to catch fish and hunt
They became a tribe of bears
A family of bears

The Little Goose

Once there was a little goose
Who simply couldn't honk
The other geese tried to help him
But he could not honk
One day they all had to fly away to Canada
And the little goose had to go with them
But he lost his way when a big helicopter scared him
And he flew in the wrong direction
Suddenly he knew he was alone
And he was so frightened
He honked and was startled at his own voice
But the other geese who were worried
And had circled around the sky
Heard the little goose
And came back to get him
They told him what a wonderful honk he had
And they all flew to Canada
Together

Listening

Once there was a little elephant

His mommy loved very much

But he was always getting lost

When all the elephants went to the pond in the morning

His mommy told him she sent out sounds he could hear

He only needed to listen and learn how to make his own sounds

But he knew his mommy would find him

And he did not listen for the sounds

But one day they were out at the pond

And the little elephant wandered far away

And took a long bath in a deep pond

And only the tip of his trunk showed above the water

Suddenly he realized he was all alone

He didn't know where his mommy was

And where the rest of the elephants were

It was very very quiet in his pond

And he tried to listen

Suddenly he heard a high funny sound

And realized he could answer it

With his huge brain in his little head

He sent out sounds

And soon his mommy came

And saw his tiny trunk in the water

And wrapped him up in her own trunk

And said, "See how important it is to listen?"

A Hot Day

It's a hot day
Heat shimmers outside
The wind is still
Holding its breath
When every other afternoon
It blows wildly
Today it is quiet
Holding a hot hand
Over its mouth
Somewhere in the sky
Where wind gets its directions
Today it has been told to be still
Time out
Behind a white cloud
The feather of a bird floats by
Propelled by nothing
The trees are motionless
Even the birds are hiding in the eaves
One flies by slowly to perch on a roof
Dry and hot
Wondering
When the wind
Can come out again
To play

Summer Heat

It is summer
Wild blackberries ripen on the hillsides
My lemon tree on the balcony still has white flowers
Hoping a hummingbird will come visit
It was soaked with water this morning
But feels the heat
Stretching its leaves in lemon tree tai chi
The cactus plants are in stasis
Hibernating in the heat

Eight

It takes the sun's light eight minutes to reach us
Eight minutes to drink a cup of coffee
To get the mail
To rinse dishes
Eight minutes for a hummingbird to beat his wings 24,000 times
Eight seconds for thunder to be heard after lightning 8 kilometers
away
Eight is a magical number
Since it never ends in the Hindu-Arabic numeral
But continually loops around and around
As the sun's light never ends
Yet reaches earth in eight minutes

Distribution Should Undo Excess

.Or Shakespeare's great message in King Lear against a backdrop of war,
Another war of generosity and truth vs greed and deceit, adversaries as bedfellows:
So distribution should undo excess
And each man have enough

Says Gloucester to Edgar
When he thinks him still Poor Tom
Yet offers the most prescient message
Of King Lear
That money should be spent
So each is served and has enough
Just as the king would have his hundred servants
Equally housed with him when forced
To join his daughters
Who received his unforced gift of land and goods
It was not for his comfort
But that his servants have enough
Be housed and fed
Yet those same daughters refused the king
His loyalty to those dependent on his will
And thus began the tragic denouement of
The story of King Lear

Parts of Act IV Scene I King Lear
(After Gloucester's eyes have been gouged out by Cornwall and Regan)
Old Man: you cannot see your way
Gloucester: I have no way and therefore want no eyes; I stumbled when
I saw. Full oft 'tis seen, our means secure us and our mere defect
prove our commodities. O dear son Edgar, the food of thy abused
father wrath. Might I but live to see thee in my touch I'd say I had eyes
again...

Gloucester to Edgar as Poor Tom:
Take this purse, thou whom the heavens' plagues have humbled to all
strokes. That I am wretched makes thee the happier. Heavens, deal so
still: let the superfluous and lust-dieted man, that slaves your
ordinance, that will not see because he does not feel, feel your power
quickly. So distribution should undo excess
And each man have enough.

Goldfinch

Goldfinches explore the trees

Quick and delicate

Pecking at flowers and berries

Calling elaborate trills and chirps

Among the leaves

Bouncing among dandelions

Nesting in tiny nests

Tiny eggs for tiny balls of fluff

Born in summer

To enjoy spent blossoms

Wind-blown seeds

Catching on thistles

Like fairy food

Enclosed

Enclosed

Head in the sand

Dark

Unforgiving

Lost

Prisons

Sit with suffering

Who will come

Accompany healing

Be present

Share life with us

Who seek oasis

Witness inhumanity

See smell touch solitary

A life time of solitary will not heal

Power of witness

Creating carpet of change

Lens into wisdom

Solitary and pandemic isolation

Does not heal

Roof

The sky is marbled softly white
A foggy veil drawn over blue
Waiting to dissipate through
Sun-soaked rags of moisture
Light delicate discarded doilies
Crocheted by wind and rain
Placed once upon tiled roofs
Now standing damp, aloof
As if expecting 4 o'clock tea
Interrupted by the wind
Blustering uninvited in
With leaves piled chattering
In break-out nattering groups
Discussing all the summer scoops
Of news on viruses and things
Of riots, cabbages and kings
Then drifting noisily away
To circle back another day
While sky and doilies mark the time
And evening settles with a rhyme

Tribes of the Torah and Beyond

We remember Adam and Eve
Abraham and Sarah and Hagar
Isaac and Rebekah, daughter of Bethuel
Who lived childless twenty years
Until she bore twins
Esau and Jacob
Esau first while Jacob held the heel of his foot
Esau born to hunt and work the land
Jacob to cultivate the gardens at home
Esau came home from work hungry
Jacob brought him potage in return for Esau's birthright
Dressed as Esau in hirsute skins received his father's blessing
Fled to his Uncle Laban to avoid Esau's wrath
Where he met Rachel and Leah and loved Rachel
Eight years worked to win Rachel's hand
Yet was deceived and received Leah as his wife
From Leah he had four boys
Reuben, Simeon, Levi and Judah
Later more children from Rachel
And their maidservants
From Levi came Moses and Aaron
And from Judah's offspring through Rebekah came
Solomon, David and Jesus
And from other offspring of Jacob and Rebekah came lost tribes
Lost as detached migrants, wandering souls
Remnants of history, tucked in rags of wisdom
Carpets of a lost people
A floor for civilization
And persecution
Carpets of history and genius
Upon which the prophets descended from Judah
David, Solomon and Jesus

Strew seeds of western civilization
Spiritual paths, music and art
Together with the legacy of Africa
Journeying through the Mediterranean
To tangle all DNA of Homo Sapiens and Neanderthal
All with stories of man made from earth
Joined through fibers and roots
Stories from Africa Asia Iceland Siberia the new world
Lakes and oceans giving birth to humankind and all life
Civilization and sorrow

Trump Pardons Susan B. Anthony

Why pardon Susan Anthony

Who reviled the law that disenfranchised her

Who repudiated the law that prohibited her vote

Who instead should be commended

For walking through the veil of injustice

For climbing through legal bars

Holding women from voting

For being arrested and fined $100

One hundred fifty years ago

$100 she would never pay

For refusing to abide by an unjust law

Would never pay for civil disobedience to injustice

Would never ask pardon

Never accept pardon

For exercising her right as a citizen to vote

Pandemic Passion (For those who live in solo bubbles)

We now must feel with our eyes
Express love with voice behind a mask
Enclosing our nostrils and cheeks
An eyebrow above partially enclosed eyes
We touch with thought
A moment of zoom behind a plastic screen
A smile caught where never begins
Wanting to walk into a zoom screen just to say Hi!
Remembering how our cat used to
Think the TV screen cat was real
Until she learned it had no warmth
It did not pounce or play
Our zoom faces smile out from images
Yet they are cold, dispassionate
One dimensional, lacking body
They can disappear with a click of a finger
They have no blood, no salt tears to taste
We do not feel their pain behind plastic
All we can share with them is a screen
With a manuscript or photo image
Created or saved by a computer program
No more or less real than the human image projected
That can be erased by clicking the icon of a camera
A voice muted by the image of a microphone
A person disappearing behind zoom
Wondering when touch will again be real
When caress more than an idea
The comfort of a hug no more forgotten
The warmth of two bodies remembered
Shared joy in together touching
More than an elusive dream
Love finding form again
As reality arises slowly from the veil of fog
Leaving behind the miasma of pandemic
And a kiss is again full of magic
And arms again full of warmth

Bird Evolution

Golden finches bounce and balance among twigs

And green shoots

Small soft bodies

Sprung from dinosaurs long ago

Bony aggression

Evolved to gentle bouncing bodies

Pterodactyl to tiny feathers was one story

Science told another later

Giving birds feathered theropods

As their weightier ancestors

Dinosaurs none the less

Unique ancient cousins

Who ate meat and surely

Could never bounce and balance among twigs

Nor chirp sweet finch songs

Nor hatch their giant eggs

From tiny nests

Superstition and Love

The psychologist Skinner

Discovered that pigeons

Are somewhat superstitious

When they receive food

They repeat the action

That preceded the reception

Bob twice, make a circle

Clockwise or counterclockwise

Hope for the reward

Unfortunately, it doesn't always work

As with us poor humans

The only assurance of reward

The only causal result

Emanates from concerted action

Grounded in skill or trust

As in love

Emanating only from love

Random love

Does not exist

Without committed love

Bobbing one's head three times

And walking sideways three steps

Won't help

Remembrance of You

Symphony in a cup of tea
Sunset on the sand
Flowing meadows full of flowers
In a petal in my hand
Remembrance of touch
In my pocket full of you
The first wisps of dawn
Your smile blowing through
A secret kept in morning light
Too brilliant for its grace
Laced fingers in a summer night
Full of stars and space

A Kiss

Gentle moment of touch
A petal loosed from its blossom
East wind forgetting its way
Glad to be lost
Among aromas of peach
And the sweet citrus of lemons
Lingering warmth
Slender trunks of budding trees
Wound about flowering yellow and blue
Arms of silk stretching into softness
Disappearing into one embrace

303

Enigma

Do I know you through mystery
Or knowledge
Through thought or intuition
Shared ideas
Shared ignorance
Shared wisdom
Shared failure
Do I know you through touch
Or turning away
Can I find you in pieces of thought
Or are we both whole
Riding on remnants of ideas
Knotted together
By a fairy goddess
To create
Our own magic carpet

The Owl and the Squirrel

The owl asked the squirrel
Are we compatible?
We both live in this tree
And never argue
But we are very different
You have fur and I have feathers
You store nuts
And I store ideas
So I can be wise
Yet what good is wisdom
If I need to forage every day
For food?
Once you told me
We were not compatible
And I thought that meant
We were no longer friends
And I pondered that a long time
Thinking I was not at all wise
To lose your friendship
I wondered if I learned to store things
You might think we were compatible
And could be friends again
But I never asked you
And storing things
Was hard for me
I think to be compatible
You should store nuts
For the winter
And I should learn
To be wise

Do We Know?

Scientists say we know when we have died

How long do we know?

And do we really?

Are there ghosts?

Can Mozart hear his music even now?

Do we know within our bodies

Are we abstracted from the physical

Merely spirits or more than merely

Perhaps greater essences

Spinning within a totality of nature

Cosmic creatures beyond reality

Earthly concerns become trivialities

Politics like pebbles

Of little consequence

Pandemics and protests

Played out on an open stage

Revealing ignorance

Transparent to a fault

Judging us as flesh or spirit

Having played our part in creation or destruction

Healing or hate

We watch the action

Viewing it as the living or as spirits

Among an audience of angels

Waiting for the curtain to fall

Prime Relationships

Some feel prime relationships

Are like prime rib

Delicious but perishable

Expendable

Friendship like a tree

Beginning with a sprout, a smile

Requiring sun and water

As it grows, its limbs remaining

Steadfast and strong

Requiring only a little attention

And few demands on time and devotion

Or is every relationship

Potentially a special friendship

Delicious

Worthy of

Preserving

Not inevitably like prime rib

To be placed in the freezer

Iced and stored

Then restored

On a whim

Unfrozen

Some other day

Or left frozen in place

An unmelted brick

Of forgotten

Memories

An incomplete idea or

Conversation

Closed behind a door

To a cold hidden closet

Full of ragged beginnings

Unfinished paragraphs

Incomplete fantasies

And frozen dreams

If I were to choose

I would choose love

Unperishable

But always leave the closet

Just a bit ajar

For air

And friendship

Pluto

Today I learned that Pluto
Has been reinstated as a planet
Along with nearly 300 other bodies
Now considered planets
What's in a name
It's all the same
As long as you are flowing in an orbit
Far from home
Gertrude Stein would have such fun
With naming planets
As they run about a universe of questions
Far more prescient
When a planet known as Pluto
Once upon a time and now
Demands that we allow
It some respect
Regain its name as we inspect
Its surface and find life
Microbial life and would you know it
Water water all around
And lots of freezing ice
Oh Pluto if we'd only known
How wonderful you are
We'd never have divorced you
From our galaxy at all

Tenderness of Air

She dreamed she taught him tenderness
Last night
It was a funny dream
They both had masks
And had to make excuses
For denying quarantine
Decided they'd been quarantined
For six long months
And had seen no one
In at least two weeks
Less than six feet away
A tutorial in tenderness
Should be okay
And so they kissed
Not to seduce
Not even to be close
Though close they were
And learned that hugs have life
Demand response
But are a momentary thing
Each touch each kiss
Each soft caress
Is simply what it is
Demanding nothing
And dreams are only air

Pretend

When in times of isolation

We need tenderness

We could play music or write a poem

When we need friendship

Dance, sing or write a story

Take a walk

Look at birds

And be reminded

They are not alone

They fly together

Nest together

So just pretend

The world is out there

Holding you as well

Boiling Water

So many angry voices on the street
Frustration contained like a pot lid
On boiling water
Spilling over scalding screaming
Voices of despair
Anguish in a teaspoon
Just a spoonful of honey
Or a cupful of money
Vapid antidotes to pain
Rebuke attempts to calm
Where is that balm in Gilead
To make the wounded whole
To sooth the human spirit
Aching to feel, to meet
To seek to find a soul
By touching humankind
To find our home
Embrace our own
Holding another's hand

Goose and Gander

The goose loved her gander

He told her once

If she left him

He would fly to the ends of earth

To find her again

They flew together

Many years

Loved and loving

Until one day

The gander folded his wings

A last time

And the goose flew

To the ends of the earth

To find him again

But flew alone

Following her lodestone

And did not find him

Until one day

She folded her wings

One last time

And found him again

Forever

Labor Day

Once upon a time
Workers clocked 12 hours a day 7 days a week
Children of 5 and 6 worked
Despite laws prohibiting child labor
Conditions were unsafe
Mills mines factories
Low wages
10,000 bricklayers, cigar makers, dressmakers, shoemakers and printers
Went on strike September 5, 1882
Marching 7 miles from New York City Hall to an uptown park
Many smoking cigars
May 11, 1894, a century after the first labor union was created
Pullman employees went on strike
Protesting cuts to wages, lining of pockets of employers
And firing of union representatives
When Debs called a boycott of Pullman cars in June
The federal government dispatched troops
At President Cleveland's command
More than a dozen workers died in Chicago
A foretaste of federal power unleashed on the people
Boycotts and protests continued
Labor Day became a national holiday June 28, 1894
Congress and Cleveland on the same side of history
To be celebrated the first Monday of September
But not till the 1900's did laws address child labor
And employee rights and wages
And even today women and minorities
Struggle to keep up with rights and privileges
Considered as the provenance of white men
And corporations continue to wield inordinate power
Blessed by the Supreme Court in its decision Citizens United
Allowing unlimited funding for political campaigns
While the President of the US through Executive mandate
Attempts to weaken the US Post Office during a pandemic
And we the people celebrate Labor Day
And hope for the best

Hot Day in the City

The sky is shimmering today

The air speaks in waves

Wrapping the city in heat

Enough to fry an egg

Or bake a cookie

On someone's rooftop

Sunday in the park

Masks mandatory but hot

Distancing more difficult

In a crowd

Even swimming a problem

No masks

Distancing difficult at the shoreline

Yet the heat still shimmers

Radiating off roofs

The birds have not found

Their birdbath on the balcony

Even they are hiding

Away from the heat

Out of the Ashes

The Peloponnesian war
Sparta against Athens
Played out against a backdrop
Of pandemic
Greeks crowded against city walls
Incapable of distancing
Succumbing to a horrible plague
In vast numbers
Even killing their leader Pericles
As war was fought
Greek against Greek

Yet as the century advanced
And saw the birth of Plato
Athens grew again
Out of the ashes of war and plague
To nourish the greatest western society
Yet known
While Sophocles and Aristophanes,
Walked its streets
Yet even there revolutionary thought
Was strangled with the arrest of Socrates
Who accepted his fate
And drank the fatal hemlock

The parallels today inspire

Hope for resurrection

A new birth

Out of chaos to stewardship

Of humanity

An opening for thought to walk

The streets of our vast country

Where all cultures and traditions

May mingle and debate

May find answers to climate change

May welcome truth again

Free the prophets Assange, Snowden, Manning

Abjure their imprisonment and torture

And embrace wisdom

Forgive

The dog asked the cat

Tell me what it means to forgive?

The word has for and give

Words I understand

So it's for you I give something

And that's forgive?

What do we give?

The cat replied, I'm not sure

I give purrs when I'm happy

It's for you or for others I give purrs

And everyone seems happy

Even when we were sad

So that's maybe forgive

Or when I curl up into your paws

When it's really cold outside

And I'm a little bit embarrassed

Because you're a dog

And I accidentally scratch your nose and you howl

But then you look at me and I've stopped purring

Because you're sad

And you pat my head with your paw

And I purr again

And the next day you don't even remember I scratched you

And I am still purring and you still pat me with your paw

Maybe that's forgive?

Jealousy

The moon said to the stars one night
When she was full and bright
I hope you aren't ever jealous of me
Just because I seem brighter to everyone on earth
You know you are much bigger and brighter
And if you disappeared it would make a difference
To the whole universe
I need you to keep in balance
On my teeter totter orbit around earth
Sometimes I even get dizzy
Just watching the earth turn
And it would be sad for the earth if I disappeared
But it wouldn't make much difference
To the rest of the universe
Because I can't even shine on my own
I need one of you great stars
I need the sun star and the reflection of earth
And I can be easily blotted out
From the only ones who see me anyway
Sort of like being put in a closet where it's dark
Every once in a while
Time Out and I haven't done anything wrong
So don't ever be jealous of me
I'm just the moon

Compromise

The monkey said to the elephant
You know the law of the jungle
Is eat or be eaten?
But you don't eat anything that eats
And I don't eat anything that eats
So maybe we are different
We don't even have to compromise
Which is a big word for me
Even longer than my tail
And there's another one I heard
Concession, which is just as long
To compromise you have to concede
Which is a little bit shorter word
But I think it means that
Animals that eat animals that eat animals
Sometimes have to let the other animals go
So they won't become extinct
Like fishing what you need
Hunting what you need and nothing more
But look how big you are
And you don't need to compromise by not eating
You just eat lots of grass
And I eat lots of bananas
And don't worry
About the law of the jungle

Humility

The lion said to the mouse

What does it mean to be humble?

Especially when you are king of the jungle?

Sometimes I think it's easier for you

Because you're very tiny

And the mouse answered

Wait a minute!

I'm smaller than you

But I'm bigger than the ants and the spiders

So don't be so big and haughty

About being King of the Jungle

Look how big the jungle is

You don't even know where it ends

It's kinda nice that you ask how to be humble

But you still think you're important

And so am I

And so are the ants

And the jungle is just part of more hugeness

That we don't even understand

Just don't pounce on me

Although you may do that someday

Because you have to eat

But maybe you can learn to be

Vegetarian

And still be king of the jungle

Even Stars

When I was a little girl
Dressed in balloon skirts
In pictures that make
My daughter laugh
When I was a little girl
The world was huge
Cats were closer than adults
In size
And a goose followed me around
Thinking I was family
When I was a very little girl
I laughed at everything
Because it was fun to laugh
I jumped in puddles
And ran in the rain
I felt close to flowers
And all small things
Even stars

Death Valley is Hot

In August, 2020
A month ago and this week, In September,
Death Valley was 130 Degrees Fahrenheit
Like opening an oven
Or directing a hairdryer at your face
Or maybe even just
Walking into an oven
The lowest place in Death Valley
Is over 200 feet below sea level
It can trap heat instead of water
It already hit 134 Degrees
Over a hundred years ago
In Furnace Creek, Death Valley
Heat is common in Death Valley
And in the winter it gets very cold
Today I wake to red skies
Red fog I think
In San Francisco
And wonder about heat and fires
Ice ages
And Death Valley

An Introvert Cake

Today I try to remember

Whoever I was over 70 years ago

Or even 60 years ago

I think I was like an introvert cake

With very thin extrovert frosting

Just enough to get by

In an extrovert world

Just enough to talk to people

A little bit

Just enough to listen

And then shut the door

Of my cake

Mixed metaphors

Like marble frosting

Marble doors

Keeping me

Outside myself

Two Houses

When I think I am loved
And someone says something that hurts
It's like I am living in two houses
A comfortable, loving house
And a house that is cold and needs repair
And suddenly I am outside both houses
And am taking a walk in my dreams
Fully unclothed
Naked to the world
And closed out
Of both my houses
Where pain has shut the doors

My Heart in a Box

Each of us sits in different spaces

Holding unique thoughts and memories

Each of us speaks a slightly different language

Built on singular etymologies of experience and being

I reach out to your space

I bring my heart to translate your language

Yet I must wait outside your windows

Looking into a dark space

Lights unlit

Until perhaps you notice me

Peering in or looking away to be polite

Walking up the pathway

Ringing at the doorbell

Rusted from time

I cannot hear if it rings or not

I stand at the door

With my heart in my hand

Hoping it can translate

Can understand your language

Explain to me the etymology

Of your spirit

But then I put it in a box

Leave it on the doorstep

And walk away

Skies over San Francisco

I have never seen the sky so dark and red

Over San Francisco

I walked to the roof

There the sky was yellow and dense

Fog protecting us from the smoke

Blowing from fires

Burning incessantly

Their smoke

Hanging high above the city

Imitating a fiery night

From residue of fires

Just now I begin to smell smoke

As birds finally venture out

Their little bodies no match

For smoke now filling the air

They peck a bit

Then disappear again

Shadows

My shadows follow other shadows

Arms intersect through dim streets

Where our journeys move

Where paths become forgotten

Lost in memory

Of shadows

Where light

Is a mirage

A remembered candle

On a Coca Cola bottle

Full of dripped wax

On a kitchen table

Surrounded by a young family

Singing happy birthday

Unaware of

The separate paths

Our shadows

Will follow

A Memory of Fire

It is September
Harvest time
The sky is red with smoke and fire
The west coast burns
Grapes may arrive
With powdery smoke
Remaining a part
Of the bouquet
Of vino 2020
Vineyards will be washed
With the coming rains
But the soil will still
Retain a memory of fire
Vertical integration
In the vineyards
Soil to vine to grape
Awaiting seasons
To remember
To forget

Pledge of Peace

Monsters in the murk
Of time and thought and
Shirking nothing to uncover our own ghosts
Of history, hiding in our conscience
Too aware of genocide and pain
Inflicted for no reason but our greed
For property and power on land that
Never could belong to us
Yet we have trampled with our
Manifest visions of destiny
To interpret correctly could only mean
Destiny of life and rights
For every color every race every idea
And every living thing
Yet we became marauders in the dust
Of what was never ours nor anyone's
As land and forest tree and glen
Can never be possessions save for all
Belonging to themselves and to the seasons
Fall and winter spring and summer
Flowers, fruits and animals
In equal portion to their needs
As even Eden exiled those that would not
Humble their own acts to laws of nature
Give the seeds their due the apples time
Respect the synergy of beet and lime
Of bipedal or quadrupedal, worm and bee
Manage land so it might see the sunrise
And the sunsets as did natives born upon the land
And generations come before
Bending in gratitude abjuring war
That all might live in amity

Protest and Questions

Daria Allen

One of many protestors in Portland

Sixteen years old

Inspired to act in memory of George Floyd

And all blacks who had been killed or injured by police

Felt it was her destiny to protest

Every day facing tear gas

She took to goggles and helmet

Then was sprayed with mace

By counter-protesters

And hit by police with a baton

Creating a painful welt on her back

When she tried to help a friend

Dana tried to balance school and protests

The corona virus gave her space to act

And question why injustice persists

Why police will injure rather than protect

The citizens of Portland

And their acts of free speech

Red Ghost

Wednesday a red ghost
Placed her hand upon the city
Blotting out the sun
As residue from fires
Spread north and south
No respite to be found
Between her ghostly fingers
Thursday she became
Chamelionlike keylime
And through the week
Her palms pressed ghostlike
Everywhere
Kneading out color as the sun
Retired behind grey clouds
And the city disappeared
In her arms
Today I look out as a pale ghost
Walks by on milky clouds
Carrying a huge bucket
Applying whitewash
With her enormous paintbrush
To all the buildings and trees
Outside my window

September 11, 2020

I look out my window
As if I were in a submarine
At the bottom of a milky sea
Dense fog and smoke at 7 am
Unseen workers in the street clattering
Collecting garbage
The woman in her pink quilt
Still curled on the corner
Barely to be seen while eyes burn
As she wakes into sunless smoky air
I watch for the old man
Who walks each morning at this time
I hear the fog horn in the bay
But I cannot see walkers
Masked against a pandemic
Now masked against the smoky air
Twenty years ago September 11, 2001
Our country thought it faced
An existential crisis
When twin towers collapsed
And the people inside became ghosts
Today I look out my window
As if I were in a submarine
Navigating a different
Existential crisis
Of pandemic
Fires and hurricanes
From climate chaos
And the realization of
Man's inhumanity to man
Hidden in the fog of injustice

Wild Fires in California

Twenty eight wild fires

Blaze across California

Scorching over two million acres

Hephaestus tramps unwillingly

Over homes and forests

As smoke from his anvil

Covers the land

Cupid gathers the arrows

Hephaestus has made

For him to shoot

Into the sky

Asking only

That the clouds

Bring rain

Survival through Immunity

We hunker down in our homes
Watch the hummingbirds
Flash by our windows
Walk in the streets with masks
Making half circles around others
Listen to the news on vaccines
Think of herd immunity
Or beehive immunity
Since bees live for the hive
We are learning to protect each other
Gradually, by wearing masks
By social distancing
Needing to trust each other
A hard lesson nature teaches us
Sending random antibodies
Each a separate set
Like a unique draw of cards
Antibodies against unknown diseases
Insurance that someone somewhere
In the human race
Will have antibodies to fight something new
A different SARS or Covid-20 or 21
Vaccines raise our chances
To protect others if not ourselves
We get flu shots to protect the vulnerable
We get Pertussis shots against whooping cough
To protect babies
Who cannot be vaccinated until they are one
Already past the danger threshold
We protect the weakest
As does nature
So that we as a human family will survive

Embrace

Embracing
Is like coming home
A bear hug
Like entering a cave
With a fire burning
Knowing you belong
You have a place
At the fire

Playing with Snakes

Ophidian miasma
Slides across our city
Aedine irritation
Aedis smirks
Gotcha!

Duck Duck Day

The ducks were in an uproar
They heard Columbus Day
Had become Indigenous People's Day
They had had enough of Columbus
Although some had come in with the
Nina, the Pinta and the Santa Maria
And were happy no one had cooked them
On board the ships
But still, they wanted more respect.
They had been around a lot longer than any human beings.
Heck, or maybe Quack,
They'd been around before the dinosaurs
Their grandparents went back 66 million years
They like to say the Mesozoic
Although that is a difficult word to quack
Duck anthropologists had found their bones in China
Could even find webs between their toes
110 million years old. Quack!
The ducks are very proud of their legs
Which grow almost under their tail
And make them waddle on land
But paddle on lakes where they swim and sleep
And all their feathers they grow on their own backs
See who can match that besides the birds!
So the ducks were in an uproar
And vowed to make a big display
When all ducks might be honored
They'd call it Duck Duck Day

They'd heard of Duck Duck Go and thought
They'd advertise it there
And when the day came, bright and fair
They gathered on their pond
And quacked and quacked and made a fuss
And started a parade
To which the cormorants and herons joined
You know how they can scream
Around the pond they went ten times
Until the bipeds came
And took some ducky pictures
And posted them online
And yelled and sang with all the ducks
And threw out special seeds
The ducks could forage on the pond
And hunt among the reeds
So don't forget to celebrate
Duck Duck day far and near
And maybe Duck Duck Day
Will be a holiday every year

Climate Chaos September 2020

As the dark skies of California

Began to clear

 Oregon held its breath

That the fires were dying out

And Washington prayed for rain

Yet across the globe

Sandstorms plunged Turkey into darkness

After thunder and lightning storms

Pushed wind to northern Turkey

And submerged Ankara in sand

Then back across the Atlantic

Florida prepared for hurricanes

To batter the gulf

And the earth turned

The pandemic raged

And birds still sang

A Foggy Sunday Morning

A foggy Sunday morning in San Francisco
I can see four lights on in a tall building
Across the street at 6 am
I wonder about four lives or four families
Beginning a day in the city
A strange city where people do not meet
Casually anymore
A strange city in a strange world
Where a pandemic takes precedence
I think of my mother speaking of the city in awe
As a place where you always dress up
And never wear white
But that was almost a hundred years ago
A different San Francisco
Lady by the bay
Dressed to the nines
Today isolated from the world
Even airplanes cannot fly her
Across the ocean
She will not be waiting for a van
At this early hour
To take her far away
Lady by the bay
You awake to fog you know so well
The four lights in one of your buildings
Begin your day in a corner of your city
Not yet dressed, not yet ready
Begin a day my mother
Would never believe
Or understand

Independent

Today I read the pandemic may never end
We must learn to live our lives in isolation
Or discover new rules to live with each other
Perhaps we will learn to make choices
We never had to make before as even now
We wear masks when we meet parents or children
To avoid sharing a virus which knows no bounds
We stay alone or learn to choose eternal loyalties
To take the time to quarantine with those we love
Make choices we had never considered
When we could spring about the web of family and friends
And there was no contagion that could kill
None that we knew of and could avoid
What new rules must we find in poetry and art and people
To access and inform our lives within new limits
Understand the value of each moment each friend each gesture
Learn how to say I love you with the squint of an eye
To laugh with the gesture of a hand
Or choose to zoom our way through life
Forgoing intimacy so as to remain free
And yet remaining tied to isolation
Independent without warmth
Independent without kisses independent in one's own cocoon
As Colette spent her last years with the company of one
Purple candle

Diversity

Our dog used to howl with the coyotes

They invited him to howl with them

Perhaps they thought he was lonely

Perhaps they wanted a new friend

A little diversity

A new voice

We could always hear him

Trying so hard

To sound like a coyote

When he howled

Afraid the coyotes

Would laugh at him

For being different

Feng Shui

Wind and water

Feng shui

Balance the world

Yet wind cannot blow away pandemics

Nor water eliminate wildfires

Wind and water

Life force

Not antidotes to nature's fist

Nor subservient to human wishes

Earthquakes

Tsunamis

Wildfires

Floods

Diseases

Fire wants to run uphill

Water wants to fill valleys

Earthquakes continue to mold earth

Pandemics inform an intersection

Between wildlife and humanity

Asking us to respect

Asking us to honor

Asking us to acknowledge nature

As Feng Shui

Wind and water

Balance the world

Covid and School

Clusters of Covid

In opening universities

Who struggle with opening campuses

During a pandemic

Students attend and become ill

Or are forced to isolate

Return home where they have lost jobs

To return to schools that again close

Due to clusters of Covid

Must juggle objects of a pandemic world

Wanting to graduate

Missing social activities

Now home

Back to parents

Wanting to grow up

In the midst of a pandemic

While some parents

Teaching elementary school or middle school

Feel threatened by coronavirus

As teachers test positive

And return home from the classroom

Perhaps teach remotely

And consider how society will heal

As a president tells us

It's all a hoax

Forum for the President

Allowing our president to speak

Encouraged by the media to create ratings

Where people will watch even to enjoy the danger and the anger

Is to allow and encourage misinformation from an alternative
reality

Press blessing of lies by broadcasting falsehoods

Horserace coverage

Who will win? Who will lose?

People's agenda coverage asks what we need to know

To make intelligent decisions

Can the press piece together priorities to ask candidates to
address issues?

Support the people's agenda or the horserace where lies are no
longer penalized

And commercial interests determine press coverage

Where the president is the major source for information about
the president

A fascist agenda a totalitarian agenda

No push back from congress gives the president an open playing
field

Where junk stories are welcomed and floods of junk cause press
chaos

Unlimited junk crowds the channels

Blots out the sky of truth

Where are the commissions to examine global failings?

To examine bounties for murder of soldiers?

To examine global interference in elections?

We await debates where the president may spew nonsense

And not be interrupted for fear of retaliation

What happened to fact based debates?

Values of a democratic society?

The purpose of press to support truth as truth?

Not to be categorized as taking sides

The press assumes traditional roles

To report presidential comments as newsworthy

Even when corrupted by intentional lies

Encouraging illegal or fatal behaviors

Vote twice

Try to dismantle the post office

Inject disinfectant to fight corona virus

Create so much untruth

So much distortion

That press and people give up

And power rules

With Fox news

What about QAnon?

What about troubles of the people?

How can we find an oasis where truth exists?

A Finch

A finch sings at my window
His wings sparkling against the sunlight
His orange head and chest
Bobbing among green lemon blossoms
He sings of love and freedom
Of joy in blue skies
And ragged clouds

A Tern

A tern was found
With banded leg
Fifteen years old
Alone with ruffled feathers
New to the lagoon
On his way farther south
A Caspian tern
Fishing for his supper
In a lagoon by the bay
Under a blue sky
And fresh air
Just cleared of smoke
From wildfires
In California
In September

Floods in the Gulf

Floods devastate Georgia

In the aftermath of Sally

Beating down on Florida

And the Gulf of Mexico

Whipping the Sandy Crane

Who seek shelter in

Crevices of cliffs

Along the shore

There is no shelter

For the ICE detainees

The women who have

Been abandoned

After forced hysterectomies

Or forced abortions

Children left to die of sepsis or flu

In unhygienic conditions

At an unforgiving border

Now facing the devastation

Of hurricanes and floods

And abandonment

Polar Bears

Polar bears migrate
To Churchill Manitoba
October every year
To wait for the Hudson
To freeze over
Where they will fish
Through the winter
Churchill even has a
Polar bear jail
For frisky polar bears
Just to keep them safe
Until the big freeze
When they will
Walk and fish
The Hudson River

Emancipation Day January First, 1863

Black Lives Matter
Needs their day to commemorate
Their unfinished emancipation
To commemorate the aftermath
Of slavery the aftermath of segregation
The aftermath of Selma and wage wars
The unfinished aftermath of discrimination
The unfinished aftermath of forced migration
From their homes in Africa
Of forced slavery in homes
On lands they did not choose
The humility of being bartered and sold as property
Of being forced on board ships in inhumane quarters
Kings and priests in Africa
Engineers and cooks
Mothers and children
Taken from their homes in Africa
Forced on ships in tight quarters
Where they might die of disease
Or malnutrition
And no one cared
Black Lives Matter
Should be remembered
On January First
With fireworks displaying
The continent of Africa
To honor those who suffered
To honor those we remade as
Ripped up roots of human life
Thrown into the pit of slavery
To feed the capitalist yearnings
Of a white people for domination

Incompatible Towhees

Said one bird gently to the other
You are a towhee and so am I
But do we fit like sugar and pie?
Maybe I could build a nest with you
Ii really like your feathers too
But what about that pretty bill
Would you rub my feathers till
They're really plush and ruffly then
I'd know that you could be my friend
The towhee tried then hard to do
Some kind of scratch but finally flew
Into the sky not knowing why
The towhee seemed to say goodbye
She thought that he was really cute
And hoped he liked her little toot
But he thought she looked like a gull
Totally incompatible
Plus he knew towhees mate forever
He'd had enough of that endeavor
And so he flew up way up high
Into the welcoming blue sky
Away from her sweet perky song
Her tweets he thought were way too long

Supreme Court Justice, Brooklyn born Ruth Bader Ginsburg, the second woman appointed to the Supreme Court, and a tireless advocate for justice and gender equality, deeply venerated for her integrity and indefatigable scholarship and grit, is profoundly mourned, having died Friday night, September 18, 2020 at age 87.

Her dying wish was that she not be replaced at the Supreme Court until after the next president was inaugurated.

Ruth Bader Ginsburg

Mentor

Advocate for justice

Advocate for women's rights

Took her place among those

Most vocal and steadfast

In demanding women's position be honored

As in the Great Laws of our indigenous peoples

She would have concurred

Women should lead us to peace and harmony

Now she rests after 87 years, after a life

Standing up for the vulnerable, women, immigrants,

For all who cried out for an advocate

Her candle will always burn in the hearts and minds of those

Who yearn that the scales be balanced

For truth and honesty

Who demand that Justice Ginsburg

Never be forgotten

Jovita Idar (1985-1946)

The New York Times recognized her as "overlooked"
She would be 135, Sept. 7, 2020
In 1914, Idar stood alone
In front of her newspaper El Progreso
Against Texas Rangers on their horses
Who would shut her newspaper down
For demanding federal troops
Vacate Veracruz and the Texas Mexican border
In response rangers destroyed the press
But not the determination of Jovita Idar
To promote education and equality for women
And all Mexican Americans
She fought to give them the free education that was their due
Ensconced in law but not reality
Finding schools without pencils, paper, books, chairs, desks
And without power to change
Jovita Idar joined her brothers at her father's newspaper
To fight against signs "No Negroes, Mexicans or dogs allowed"
To fight against inadequate schools
And poor living conditions for Mexican Americans
Against discrimination and inequities
As first president of the League of Mexican Women
She brought Mexican American rights into focus
And women's rights
Helped pass the Nineteenth Amendment
To give women a vote and representation
First defeated when put to the male vote in 1919
Then passed, June of that year
Jovita Idar spent her life fighting for Mexican American rights
For women's rights
With her pen and voice
Fighting to transform society into one of justice for all

Within Your Heart

The years go by
Souls disappear
You lose a voice
You used to hear
Each day each moment
Half of you was hidden
In a voice so dear
You hear it still
Within your heart
That voice, its face
Are still a part
Of who you are
And whom you love
Like fingers resting in a glove
That holds you gently
Holds you tight
Yet lets you rest within a light
So warm it comforts
Deep inside
Becomes your compass
And your guide
Your path
So you may never cease
To seek his spirit
And your peace

Snakes

Are we surprised?
The president tells us ballots are unnecessary
That we are not looking at an election
But a continuation of power
We don't really need the post office
Even the Voice of America is politicized for the president
The police who shot Breonna Taylor in Kentucky
Are neither condemned nor convicted
In protests, police ride their bicycles over a man's head
A truck hits a protestor while driving into the crowd
Two reporters are arrested for covering protests
We look back at the last few years
Government shutdowns
Presidential impeachment
Global pandemic
Economic recession with depression-era levels of unemployment
Overdue national push-back against race police brutality murder
Tension with China Iran and our allies
Coupled with insouciance towards climate change
Ensuing tornadoes wildfires floods murder- hornets locusts
The death of John Lewis and the last blow
Losing Supreme Court Justice Ruth Bader Ginsburg to cancer
A level, moral voice on the court
Her cancer as with our plague and protests
Symbolic of the demise of America
Are we surprised and can we rectify the damage?
Can poetry elicit change
Word by word
Idea by idea
Book by book
The world is our oyster
Consumed by snakes

I am a Vaquita (a small porpoise)

I am a vaquita

I just learned there are only ten of me

I am a little porpoise

Who lives in northern Mexico

It's hard for me to find friends

My family pals together

But there aren't very many of us

It's hard to give a party

So we just swim around

In the Gulf of Mexico

We dive and splash

But we aren't getting any younger

And I hope we'll be okay

Sunset and the Face of the Moon

The sunset was streaks of red and gold tonight

While in the east the pasty moon had waxed nearly round

She floated very prettily behind her foggy veil

Almost indistinguishable from the sky itself

Just a chalky face

Floating in the fog

Haiti, Land of the Mountains

Haiti, land of the mountains
Haiti, land of the Taino
Land of restorative justice
Land of suffering
Land of rape and pillage
Gifts of the Spanish, the French, the Americans
A land whose stories do not end in justice or moral lessons
A land whose stories end in blood
A land who remembers the Taino maiden from Boriken
Who washed her father's rainbow belt by the river
When a Spaniard on a horse saw her beauty
Killed her father with his huge white dog
Raped her brutally and cut off her head
So her body would be unrecognized
The Taino lived peaceably
In the Caribbean
Always peaceably
Among enemies who enslaved them
Enslaved them to work the plantations
Until one day in Haiti,
An enslaved people
Repudiated their slavery
And won their independence
Only to be punished again
Indentured by the powerful colonialists

Made to pay blood money for their bodies and labor

Oh unhappy imperialists with slaves

Worried that a free Haiti

Would corrupt other slave economies

With the wish for freedom

Oh let us cut off the head of Haiti

So the ownership of its beauty may not be recognized

Its people unrecognized, anonymous

Punish its arrogance

The arrogance of a savage, invisible island people

Rape its soul, rape its land, its forests

Pollute its waters

Rain horror on its people in the city and land of the sun

Till there is nothing left but disease and poverty

In a gentle people's paradise

Do I hear Drums in Haiti?

Do I hear drums in Haiti?

A heartbeat pounding out blood and heat

Pumping joy and melancholy

Blood flowing to the sea

Washing through the corals

Singing of its source

Do I hear drums in Haiti?

Chanting of its soul

Voodoo introspection

Singing sun and sand

Do I hear drums in Haiti?

Drumming from the mountain

Carried by the beetle

Trembling rhythmically

A beat of ancient legend

Jazz and folklore

Song and story

Chanting rocks and reeds and fountains

Chanting birds and blood and mountains

Chanting birds and blood and mountains

Do I hear drums in Haiti?

The Haitian Princess

A Voodoo princess sits upon the mountain

Dressed in green

Her legs stretched wide

Reach to the horizon

As waters swell within her fertile womb

Her soul dances to the song of the whistling frog

And laughs with its ventriloquist colleague

Creating a tapestry of music

In seven note chirps long and distant

Thrown like gossamer petals

Above her green mountain tresses

Looped in orchid dreadlocks

Roque Dalton, Martyr (San Salvador, El Salvador, 14 May 1935 – Quezaltepeque, El Salvador, 10 May 1975)

He was killed by his brothers, his friends, his fellow rebels

He wrote of the poor who lived on anything and nothing

Of death in love rather than death in hate

Those who feared the poet threatened him

With the slander of betrayal

Threatened to smear his red ghost

The ghost that died betrayed

O Roque, you knew the sounds of nature

Crickets and growing things

In fields of El Salvador

You knew the sounds of crying babies

Encircled by massacring armies

Hiding in those same fields

Starved as their mothers died

Killed as they screamed

You knew the sounds of hate

And the sounds of love

You knew Cuba

You knew Prague

You knew Diego Rivera

You knew revolution

And you were a poet

A soldier of truth

Killed for your belief

In life and justice

Roque Dalton, Martyr (San Salvador, El Salvador, 14 May 1935 – Quezaltepeque, El Salvador, 10 May 1975) Translation into Spanish by the author

Fue asesinado por sus hermanos, sus amigos, sus compañeros rebeldes

Escribió sobre los pobres que vivían de todo y de nada

De la muerte en el amor en lugar de la muerte en el odio

Los que temían al poeta lo amenazaron con la calumnia de la traición

Amenazado con manchar su fantasma rojo

El fantasma que murió traicionado

O Roque, conociste los sonidos de la naturaleza

Grillos y cosas que crecen en campos de El Salvador

Conocías los sonidos de bebés llorando

Rodeados por ejércitos masacradores

Escondidos en esos mismos campos

Murieron de hambre mientras sus madres murieron

Muertos mientras gritaban

Conocías los sonidos del odio

Y los sonidos del amor

Conocías Cuba

Conocías Praga

Conociste a Diego Rivera

Conociste la revolución

Y eras poeta

Soldado de la verdad

Asesinado por tu fe en la vida y la justicia

El Polin Spring

There's an old legend that says if a woman drinks from the naturally-occurring fresh waters of El Polín Spring under the full moon, she'll have many children and a long life. The myth was widely circulated in the 19th century among the soldiers of the early Spanish Presidio, which in those days encompassed a small site just to the spring's northwest. The Ohlone used to live close by in a village called Petlunec near what is now Chrissy field.

In 1776, the Spanish established their fort or "presidio" within walking distance of El Polín Spring. **Juana Briones** lived here as a young girl. I visit there often to see the birds and butterflies, the trees and flowers and the spring and ruins of the old village. I think it's an important part of our Mexican history and heritage.

El Polin Spring

I walk across a spring
Discovered by natives in a forest
Centuries ago
Home to butterflies and birds
Home to lupine and lilacs
Home to a quiet breeze
And hidden shelters
Under native trees
I walk across a spring
And look up at hills and forest
Circled by large birds
Serenaded by warblers and jays
See hummingbirds whirr
And dash upwards like tiny rockets
I walk across a spring
And admire stone benches
And foundations of a village
Sheltering peoples of a past time
Whose shadows still evoke
Ghosts of a spirit world meditating
At a rippling spring
Where warblers and woodpeckers
Still bear testimony to their ancient memories

Translation into Spanish by the author
Poem on El Polin Springs Poema El Manantial El Polin

Voy a leer mi poema sobre el primer a sentamiento mexicano en California
El Manantial El Polin en el Presidio
Hay una vieja leyenda
Si una mujer bebe en los manantiales frescos bajo la luna llena, tendrá muchos
hijos y una larga vida.
Los soldados del presidio español conocían la historia.
El manantial estaba a poca distancia
Juana Briones vivió allí de niña. Es una parte importante de la herencia
Mexicana

El Manantial El Polin

Camino por un manantial
Descubierto por los nativos en un bosque
Hace siglos
Hogar de mariposas y pájaros
Hogar de lupino y lilaca
Hogar de una brisa tranquila
Y refugios ocultos
Bajo árboles nativos
Camino por un manantial
Y mira las colinas y los bosques
Rodeados por grandes pájaros
Con serenatas de currucas y arrendajos
 Escucho zumbidos de colibríes
Y veo se lanza hacia arriba como pequeños cohetes
Camino por un manantial
Y admirar los bancos de piedra
Y los cimientos de un pueblo
Albergando a personas de un tiempo pasado
Cuyas sombras aún evocan los fantasmas de un mundo espiritual
Meditando en un manantial donde las currucas y los pájaros
Carpinteros
Aún dan testimonio de sus antiguos recuerdos

Extinction

Dinosaurs walked into extinction
Without human intervention
Without human pollution
Without human destruction of their forests
Dinosaurs were perhaps too big
To survive naturally contaminated air
Filled with methane residue
Or perhaps too big to survive on depleted vegetation
Or perhaps, as science fiction writers conjecture
They were destroyed by a passing meteor that exploded on earth
Today even without a passing meteor
They would probably not survive humanity
As we destroy species after species
As we destroy rainforests
And contaminate our air with smoke
As we destroy insects
Our insurance policy for survival
As we destroy bees
Through pesticides and carbon
Though greenhouse gases
It is said when bees disappear
Life on earth disappears
Our pollinators
Creators of honey
Sustaining birds and insects
Must survive or with their loss
A land of milk and honey
Scriptural metaphor
For heaven
And survival
Disappears

Spirit Love

Joy laughter delight sorrow

Childhood memories flowing warmth

Global tenderness

Smiles for children

Reaching beyond masks

Reaching beyond distancing

Reaching beyond worry of contagion

Flying without thought of time

Being nature

Being the rose

Being the call of the bird

Carrying sorrow

Carrying hope

Carrying breath

All the while distant

All the while masked

All the while

A spirit

Beyond touch

Yet present

Beyond speech

Yet listening

Beyond air

Yet everywhere

Spirit love

Track the Sound of Light

Track the sound of light
The taste of lightning
The smell of air under a daffodil
In a field far away
Taste the song of a bird
Hear the beauty of its wing
Flying into the dying rays
Of a sunset
Feel the thunder
Echoing through the ages
As lightning pierces
Every soul you have known
Since childhood
Hide those souls
Within your sleeves
Where you are growing orchards
Full of flowers

The Monkey and the Parrot

The monkey said to the parrot
The lions are making fun of us
Because we're always together
I don't like to be humiliated
Just because you hang out with me
To which the parrot replied
The lions are jealous
Because we are friends
And we can fly and climb
They can't do that
The lions don't have many friends
Because they eat everything
They like to eat animals with brains
We like seeds and bananas
Fruit and leaves and bark
And we don't eat anything that thinks
Or talks or sings
At least I don't think so
And lions just roar
And want to be king
But I can talk
And you can chatter when lions are around
So we can be careful
But we're so different from each other
Said the monkey
To which the parrot squawked
We can help each other
And learn from each other
Let the lions make fun of us
Who cares?
And the little monkey climbed on the parrot
And away they flew

Heat

Heat bounced off the windows across the street

Sending waves of warmth curling around passers by

Walking slowly through hot city streets

Seeking in vain for shadows

Or a breeze

To remind their faces of air

Even the trees were silent

Leaves hanging suspended in stillness

Hummingbirds shot upwards

Making their own tiny wind

Catching insects who were not wary

And the sun blazed down

Somewhat apologetic

For her unveiled fire

While the fog hid in the waters of the bay

Fearing the heat

Ancient Autonomies of the Caucasus

Abkhazia, South Ossetia, republics fleeing domination

Now Nagorno-Karabakh

Historically the Kingdom of Artsakh

One of the last medieval Armenian kingdoms

To remain independent until the Turks invaded

Leaving it open to rule by Mongols, Turks, Persians, Russians

And in 1920 the Soviet Union

Who at dissolution forced it to join Azerbaijan

Artsakh –some still say Nagorno-Karabakh

Once a refuge for Christians and persecuted minorities

For Armenians fleeing genocide by the Turks

Little countries squeezed between historic powers

Retain pride of ancient cultures and language

Seek their own independence

From mighty Russia

Sitting on Georgia

Turkey to the west and south

Iran to the south

Among these giants

Little countries in the Caucasus

With ancient cultural roots

Seek to cultivate their own histories

Once kingdoms of art and poetry

Creating tapestries and sculpture from the earth

Sculpture Deep in the Caucasus

Defining the very mountains they embrace

Discussing poetry art and religion

Yet overrun by ambitious neighbors

Tossed between strangers

Juggled among neighbors

Who would control their riches

Their pipelines from the Caspian Sea

Tired of being a side show

Raise their heads

And smile in beauty

Trade their oranges at harvest

To those who would control them

Refuse to accept rule

By those who do not know them

And cannot tell their stories

Red Moon

Red moon floats above the horizon
Discards her veil as earth rolls over in her ancient bed
Laughing from above within a golden jewel
As fires and smoke envelope earth in red
Forests tumble and houses burn
Pandemic scourge invades the ruling few
Taking their turn at a table set for all
Passing the karma passing the right wing stew
Spices tempering the sauces and the lies
The moon looks down from black and sullen skies
Looking at a world now cast in fear
As dawn persuades the moon to disappear

A Cold Blustery Evening

A cold night
Fog descends Telegraph Hill in chilly silence
A finch seeks refuge on my window sill
Fluffing his feathers till
Too cold to chirp
She flutters to my tiny balcony
Settling lightly in the eaves
For a small reprieve
A sheltered remedy
From blustering chill

Cultivating for the Harvest

I gathered some early fallen avocados
The harvest had been rich months earlier
The old tree had tried again to produce fruit
But the timing was off
The season was past
She would have to wait until the winter had passed
She would have to wait into the next year
The avocados I gathered were tiny
I still tried to peel them, tough as they were
I cooked them with onions
Giving them a chance to be themselves
Green and rich
And they tried
But their flavor was lost
As the tree had tried to tell me
I must wait till she is ready

Sometimes we are like a tiny avocado
Impenetrable yet yearning
Remembering ripeness
On the patient tree
Full of life and joy
Now waiting for another season
To embrace the skies
To embrace the earth
To embrace life
And be held by angels

We have cultivated
We have harvested
And learned
All life has its seasons

All life requires warmth
All life must be held
Must be received when ready
When the sugars are right
When it is time to be gathered
Taken early grapes are tart yet fresh
Taken late they may be overripe yet sweet
As an elegant sauterne
From Chateau d'y quem
Yet each must be loved
For what it is or is not
All life must be cherished

Could all humanity
Be cultivated with care
Be given socks for warmth
Lying barefoot under waiting trees
Be gathered and be held
Be fed and clothed
Embraced in mutuality
As Shakespeare and Mozart
Would have all humanity
Mingle in equity
Young old sweet sour
All colors of the rainbow
All seasons of the peach or avocado
So must we cultivate each other
That we may harvest wisdom

The Moon Sails

The moon sails into the sea of the sky
Creating a wake of night fog
Etched with occasional stars
She hides behind her coastal veil
Shy yet radiant
Below her window-lit buildings compete
With squares of light
Beaming uncovered at the sidewalks and sky
As if they held truth in their lighted windows
Yet behind the glass secrets hide
Like inside fog
Secrets tucked into the cushions
Behind the bookshelves
Under the rug
Between the cups and saucers
Waiting to be held and clattered
Cleaned and scattered
Secrets and tiny falsehoods
Hoping to remain hidden
Yet wishing to be found
Wanting to be opened
Like packages of stars
Wrapped in gauze
And spun glass
Dangerous
Yet beautiful
Like the secrets
Of the moon

Katmai Alaska

Salmon have run through the rivers of Katmai
As long as she can remember
She who saw settlers arrive 5,000 years ago
To seek bear and fish her streams
To hunt the riches of nature
To escape the sudden volcanic eruptions
Still marking her history
Countless warblers, eagles and osprey
Mergansers and ducks
Tell her story on their migrations south
But always return to her welcoming forests
And the valley of ten thousand smokes
The aftermath of the Novarupta-Katmai eruption
Covering Katmai with three days of darkness
Volcanic ash and smoldering aromas
And underneath the smoldering residues
Of thousands of fumaroles
Smoking chimneys spread across the valley
Once home to the Eloquii
Now her green lushness lost to volcanic fingers
Piercing through her ancient earth
Her peoples moving with bear elk and deer
With her feathered migrants
To different twists and corners of her rivers
Where Russian entrepreneurs begged for otter pelts
From indigenous who stewarded their land
And hunted only for need
Failing to see into Katmai's misty future
The new world of exploitation
Today part of that world
Fingers rising not only from nature
But from strangers
Who do not know her story

Who do not know of her ancestral tribes
Coming from even farther north and east
To this cold volcanic Eden
To settle and hunt
To build homes encircled by trenches
To swallow the cold in front of their doors
Hung with pelts
To converse with people and spirits
Souls and immortal nature
Yupik, Aleut, Inuit or Inupiaq
To revere the medicine man Sagdloq
Who traveled to the sky and under the sea
Meditating eternally with their spirits
And with the spirit of Katmai herself
Whose people spoke Inuit and Yupik or Sirenik and Aleut
Echoes of ancient Alaska
Telling stories of other lands and her own
Her volcanoes, her rivers, her mammals, her reptiles
Her flying creatures and her salmon
Who have run through her waters
As long as she can remember
And longer still until forever

Trail of Tears

Cherokee traveled the trail of tears
Nearly 200 years ago
Uprooted from their homes in
Tennessee Alabama North Carolina Georgia
Homes where they had built villages of log cabins
Taught their children the Sequoyah alphabet
Written language of Cherokee
Lived according to the law of their constitution
Become the model for our own constitution
Which lacked only the Cherokee tribal reverence for women
Who selected their chiefs and supervised deliberations
According to the Great Law of Hiawatha and the Great
Peacemaker
Of the Haudenosaunee
This civilized people were forced from their homes
To walk to Oklahoma
Called Indian Territory
16,000 Cherokee children parents grandparents
Traveled over 1000 miles across desert and mountains
Through all seasons
Those who did not die on the trail
Often perished from relocation
Still suffer today
Robbed of their rights
So others could rob the gold of Georgia
And appropriate the property of the Cherokee
Robbed of their heritage
Those Cherokee live today in poverty
Susceptible to sickness
Especially in times of Covid
Live still in the aftermath
Of the Trail of Tears
In the aftermath of continued injustice

Don't

Don't skip
You look like a girl
Wait a minute!
An early glimpse
An early lesson in manhood
I wished my son had never had
He loved to skip
I loved to see him skip
I loved to skip too
The joy of bouncing
The rhythm of touching the pavement
With a rolling toe
Then swinging into the air
The euphoric joy of being
Of breathing in rhythm
To skipping
How human
Such genderless joy

Don't walk on the grass
Don't sit on the grass
Wrote a troll on a sign somewhere
Wait a minute!
Someone created grass
For us to lie on
For us to roll in
For us to sit and dream upon
To meditate upon
While chewing blades of grass
While rubbing dandelions
Under our own or
Our children's soft chins
Or for chasing seeds from dandelions
Blowing through green grass

Don't slam the door
Wait a minute!
Door slam themselves often enough
And children are more important
Than doors that simply
Don't know how to close quietly

Roots

Unrooted
Deracinated
Growing up on foreign soils
Children in a family
Seeking nourishment from naked roots
Stretching towards nourishment
Stretching towards home
Seeking always seeking
A language within a context
Geborgenheit
Belonging
Tendrils crawling through siblings
Stretching towards familiarity
Looking for kindred spirits
Thirsting for stories of belonging
Family histories rooted in here
Wanting a there to burrow into
To burrow into and leave and return
A space of things and ideas and people
Who write its story
Who grow its roots
Who nourish its beginnings
Who sustain its journeys
Who walk with loving ghosts
From here to there
Unrooted like flowing jellyfish
We float and seek
Our sibling
Like uprooted trees
In foreign soil
We stretch our tendrils far
To reach our family

Mexican Policy

Along the US southern border
In Matamoros, Mexico
Babies and children crowd against the Rio
Smells of urine and offal fill the air
Decapitated bodies float down the river
The same river where families must bathe
Since there are no wash stations
Tens of thousands of people
Push to these open air camps across the river from Texas
Fleeing starvation and impossible conditions
From countries strangled by the US
The richest country in the world
Tired, weak and hungry
Invisible in their desperation to all but the drug cartels
Or border police who may kidnap the women to rape
With their eyes and mouths taped shut
Or ask for ransom to return them to their children
Over two thousand who make it to the camps are children
Spending their childhood in squalor in Mexico
Because they could not stay in Guatemala, El Salvador,
Honduras
Because they were forced out of Latin countries
Once beautiful countries that were their homes
Only five in one hundred finding legal representation
From lawyers who struggle to choose whom to represent
The most vulnerable or those who have a chance to be heard
Though US policy will reject nearly all begging for asylum
Others drown trying to cross the river
Observed only by magnificent Sandy Cranes
Standing tall guarding the river
The only guardians to be trusted
As they cross the Rio on their mighty wings

Matamoros Mexico

Matamoros Mexico
Tent city on the border
Synonymous with waiting
Synonymous with suffering
Synonymous with hopelessness
As Covid shuts the doors to asylum
The magic applications
Impossible to obtain
From shuttered offices
Safety
Impossible to secure
After battering from Hanna
Leaves camps inundated
Vulnerable to vermin
Twenty bodies float in the Rio
Leaders in the camps
Victims of drug cartels
Children try to play
In filth between tents
Food and water remain scarce
And insecure
Matamoros
Symbol of decay
Of our America
Our America
Pledged to be our brothers' keeper
To welcome huddled masses
Shuts her doors
To suffering
Shuts her doors
To those whose countries
She herself exploits

Children of the Northern Triangle

A million and a half children

Cannot go to school in Guatemala

Forced into child labor

Military conscription

Trafficked into sex or war

Neither of which they understand

Asylum requests

Mostly by women and children

Increase 100 percent in ten years

In Guatemala Honduras El Salvador

These are the children who often get lost at the border

Separated from parents or simply alone

Wandering the maze of bureaucracy

Wandering the maze of an insecure childhood

Wandering a maze of violence hunger loss

Found drowned in rivers of the world

Lost in unwelcoming villages

Tiny strangers bereft of childhood

Tiny ones bereft of trust and hope

Alone in a world with no room for them

With no room for their need

For the warmth of an embrace

With no room for their yearning

For a place at the table

Of humanity

Nets of Night

The sky is skeptical
The sun indifferent
The clouds continue morphing
Into shapes to shade the earth
As gentle boats continue rowing
Over undecided dimming blue
And sunshine shrugs as she must exit
Off a softened dusky rim
While gathering modestly
Her ample skirt of red and gold
Woven by the paddles of the skies unhurried boats
Slipping Into swirls of sunset
Morphing once again
Into the nets of night

This Morning

October morning
Dark and starless
Unopened doors of fog
Still hide her secrets
Coyotes guard the silence
Quietly padding city streets
Only the rumble of a distance jet
Mars the quiet
As she seems to emulate
Yet unawakened
Hovering birds of prey

Gentle People

Gentle people trudge north
Seeking safety
Marching northward
For nearly a century now
Seeking safety from violence
Once from genocide
Then from artificial states
With artificial governments
Installed to feed a wealthy world
Arrogant protagonists of suffering
Gentle people trudge northward
Their daughters fleeing rape
Their sons fleeing conscription
To street wars over drugs
Gentle people trudge northward
Seeking safety for their children
Seeking homes where they are safe
Communities where they can work
A piece of land where they can farm
A piece of hope
Gentle people trudge away from expulsion
Into rejection
Forced back with their families
Or separated from their children
Becoming victims again
Refugees from never
Trudging into ever
Ever hoping
Ever trudging
Ever gentle

Gentle Elephant in the Room

We fight for green energy
Embraced by many as renewable
Sustainable efficient green
Yet its costly grid will never meet
Our nation's energy needs
While standing waiting for us
Is the beautiful elephant in the room
Dense efficient fourth generation nuclear power
Being developed throughout the world now
Only not in the United States
Still wedded to the idea of wind turbines
Solar panels and hydroelectric power
All requiring external energy sources to function
All breathing out a residue of pollutants
All taking space from wildlife
Immigrating birds seeking land to rest upon
Free of murderous wind turbines
Free of plants leaking methane
And producing fossil fuels
To continue to warm our world
And acidify our oceans
While the beautiful elephant in the room
Could power the whole planet
Sufficient not only to energize our world
But to begin to rid it of its plastic and spent debris

Capable of being placed anywhere

Small, dense pockets of energy

Some of which can fuel themselves

From spent fuel from old generation plants

Independent of external fuels

Free of exhaling pollutants

Small nuclear plants

Waiting for us to take them in

And give them homes

To energize the world

And allow it to cool down

Like spraying water

From an elephant's trunk

Water that might finally

Be relived of its carbon burden

Along with the air it fills

While the whole world

Will finally be able to energize

Feed and sustain itself

Like the gentle elephant in the room

Waiting for a home

Walking

You walk in the city
Pelicans fly overhead
A baby gull looks at you across the street
Sparrows trill from the bushes
And even a squirrel finds its way up a tree nearby
The vastness that is the world
The grime that is the city
Become a moment
Where you belong in everything

You walk along the shoreline
Gulls squawk and soar
Crabs find their tide pools
Hiding in the sand
While you watch their tiny scuttles
Children dig channels and castles
Digging the channels so deep
They sit in the moat
While the castle falls
You dig your toes in the sand
And become the sand
The tide pools, the scuttling crab
And the submerged castle

You walk in the ancient forest
Gazing upwards towards pieces of sky
Glancing out from tops of old redwoods
Mushrooms form a circle under your advancing feet
Crushing old leaves and pine needles
Smells of fungus and pine fill the air
You reach down to pick up a pinecone
Just small enough for a large pocket in your old coat
You hear the hammer of an industrious woodpecker
And imagine yourself in the hole he creates
Tiny and yet hiding in a hole so small
It fills all of creation

The Moon Wishes

The moon looks through my window

A waxing crescent

Lying comfortably in a velvet sky

Fog has settled on the night

Determined not to give the stars a chance

To compete with the moon

So all alone in the October sky

She glows

Hoping a bit wistfully

The stars might come out to play

Ohlone of the Bay at Hunters Point

Tidal wetlands and hills

Home to the Ohlone

Curled into a bay of clean sparkling water

Full of fish, otter, dolphins

Where bear hunted and hibernated

Coyotes howled at dusk

Squirrels hid their treasures

Sparrows, warblers, owls

Filled the air and trees

Children played and sang

Families celebrated life

Danced and beat their drums

Muwekma Ohlone were consecrated

In sacred shell mounds with their ancestors

While further generations of first peoples

Hunted, gathered and lived in peace

Generations lived and died along the coast of California

Long before the Spanish came

Yet are little remembered

While the history of butchers

Cattle shrimp shipyards and truckers

Factories and industry

Towers and facilities to bring power and

Energy to the wealthy in the upper city

Dominate memorial texts written in slabs

Upon the ancient home of the Ohlone

And a field of asphalt fills the spaces

Once rich in grasses, raccoons, opossums

Rich in fruit and corn and herbs

Now dormant like a mausoleum

Redolent with history of the Ohlone

Ignored by those who should be its protectors

Instead become a corrupt pot of gold

For those who would exploit it in the name of profit

Leave new generations of the vulnerable

To develop asthma from pollutants

Infection from disease and pandemic

New generations of dark skinned forgotten

To seek justice on this land

While the Ohlone merely seek their home

That it may teem again with fish and deer and foraging bears

In tidal wetlands and sparkling waters

Nobel Peace Prize to UN Food Program

The world is starving
Human ambition led us to this end
In the last three years
Before any pandemic
Numbers on the brink of starvation
Had risen from 80 million to 135 million
Each one a person with family children friends
Children going to bed hungry
Now with a pandemic 270 million people starving
Our planet cries
Knowing it is mother to millions who are dying
Knowing it is mother to billionaires making money
From suffering
Sometimes unaware of their responsibility
Like children who leave toys on the stairs
Ignorant of the danger to others
Billionaires leave banana peels for the world to slip upon
When all they need is food
That a few billionaires could provide
With pennies from their pockets
Money piles up
Money spent to devastate mother earth
With digging and burning of fossil fuels
Warming the earth killing her children
Sending thousands of animals to extinction
Deforestation, plastics in the ocean
Already so acidified marine life is dying
Even the plankton upon which whales depend suffocates
Mother earth weeps hurricanes and cyclones
Screams as fires burn her skin
Begs her children succor their own
Smiles at a Nobel Prize for the UN Food Program
Yet knows that is not enough
That prizes will not feed the children
Nor stop the devastation of earth
Nor even pick up the banana peels or the toys on the stairs

Pearls to Remember Water

Walking through diamonds of yesterday

Feet numb with tiny scars bleeding jasmine

Kneeling in pools of incense

Wrapping my knees in pearls

He gave me to remember water

Hands clasped over scented lilies

Making me remember tears

Damp testaments to albums of ever

Pressing like fog upon my brow

Melting as incandescent ice

Flowing with glaciers of unforgotten ideas

Yet glowing in a beating heart of silent sorrow

Tunnels open up beneath a stream of moonlight

Soon extinguished in a cascade full of stars

Beating eons circle round my head

Transfixed and staring at an unknown world

Churning through a question studded universe

Roaring voice of daffodils becoming waterfalls

Pouring through my still and silent soul

Hammering blue visions fraught with light

Pressing through a forest bed of golden

Trees of pine transformed into soft petals

Raining on my solace and my dreams

Shadows Answer

Shadows answer shadows

Candles swim through light

Moon grows upon the water

Rippling roots of brilliance

Reflecting stars mirroring the sky

Remnants of sunset fall softly

Cinderella rags transformed in magic

Roll upon the carpet of the growing moon

Reaching out for darkness on a pebbled shore

Ancient love forgets its secret

Wraps itself in sorrow

Holding water in leaking hands

Dripping tears salt upon salt

To disappear in tiny circles

Like rain on silken water

Soon to be absorbed

Beyond forget

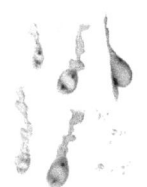

New Life for Old Ships

Microbes of sediment creep into shipwrecks
Diverse personalities of microbiomes
Gather to corrode and munch
To load rough means to eat
Marinated delicacies of wood and iron
While other microbes
Gather to protect old ships
In shallow or deep water
Covering them like a blanket
Weaving viruses and archaea into layers
Woven by angel mermaids
Murmuring lullabies to just born oysters
Mussels tiny eels and fish
Breathing reefs of social grace
Reborn nurseries from ships
Visited by humans also leaving traces
Foreign guests visiting old microbiomes
Socializing salt and seaweed
Oxygen and anaerobic micro organisms
Share their air in bubbles
Dealing cards of elements
Stacking decks of microbial bacteria
Home for tiny viruses
Builders of a new environment
Neptune in his deep sea garden
Nestling in an old forgotten ship
T'was brillig and the slithy tows
Did dance and gambol
In the ripping tides
Upon a marinated feast
While Neptune with his triton
Wisely hides

Spider Webs and Stars

A massive spider web of gas

Snuggles in a corner of the universe

Strung by fingers of god

Capturing milky ways

Six galaxies cling to gaseous threads

Spider work of angels

Woven into eons of time and matter

Singing space

Racing still through universal chambers

Munching gaseous threads

Wrapping insect yearnings

Into vast cocoons

Hanging upon web spun pockets

Heavy with dark waterfalls

Flung through mirrors of yesterday

Cracked by stars

Pandemic Poetry

How can one be a poet in isolation?
Drawing on memories becomes a new art form
The pictures one paints on memories a new kind of painting
Colors transformed by the computer to the grayscale
Sharp contrasts and gray fog
Remembered what one would forget
Lost in the fog the moments one clings to
Fingers holding on to sand
Grayscale made tangible
Then drifting into a beach of never
Ever multiple grains
Raining virtual irreality

Debate

Presidents and would-be presidents debate
Avoiding anything of substance
A bland circus of recrimination and defense
A sideshow to reality
Accusations containing their own truth
By virtue of statement
Numbers obfuscated by non-numbers
Past statements resurrected to prove nothing
But to be placed in minds out of context
Perhaps creating non-points
Unintended slips of the tongue
That could change an election

To spin

If I were to spin

Indefinitely

Infinitely

Away

Where would I go?

Would I hang upon the arms

Of a clock?

Or dissipate

In boiling rage

Spewed by volcanic fire

Creep into politicians brains

And make the thoughts

And words

That bring destruction

Or world peace?

Accumulate my molecules In Saturn's rings

Or dance upon the moon

Separate myself

In cosmic leaps

Or cling

Desperately

To the me

 Of me?

Somebody in Portland Loves Me

The large white bear looks out the window
A smaller bear, whose shirt says
"Somebody in Portland loves me"
Lies on the sofa beneath the mama bear
Both of them
Waiting for children to walk by on the street
And wave

Miracle of Meeting

There is a miracle in meeting
A miracle in touch
The warmth of a hand or a cheek
A miracle in sight
The tenderness of a look
A miracle in sound
A miracle in speech
In the texture of a voice
Unique to the miracle of meeting
For the first time or perhaps
A long time afterwards
Remembering and meeting again
A miracle

Donald and the Moonkins

A special duck with an affinity for water and space travel
Found water on the moon
Just a few weeks ago
And moonkins looking for work
Donald, we'll call him
Thought of a scheme to bring water from the moon to earth
Via magnetic straws
He suggested the moonkins become qualified
To blow the water to earth
Via magnetic straws
Recently he made his weekly trip to the moon
With zillions of straws
Which he distributed
One by one
To moonkins
Wanting to blow straws
Who had shown they were qualified
And would not litter the moon
With their unique straws
Then he took off for earth
Fastening magnetic straws
End to end all the way
But got lost
As ducks sometimes do
And wound up on an asteroid
That had just been tested by an earth robot
Donald settled in
As ducks are very flexible
In any environment
Receiving water from his straws
He created a little oasis on his asteroid
With a ducky atmosphere

With palm trees and other life forms
Sprouting up through the water
Pushed via his straw pipelines
Onto his asteroid from the moon
In a very speedy time zone
Of no time at all
With his smartphone with him
Donald signaled to Daisy and his nephews
To catch an earth robot rocket
And come visit and maybe they could all go back home
And finish the straw pipelines to earth
With magnetic straws
Hoping their pipeline would be legal
Blowing water from the moon
Via straw blowing moonkins
Who now had regular work
And Donald assured them
A living wage
Blowing water
From the moon

Milarepa Wisdom

In a great cave

High in the Himalayas

Milarepa meditated

Praying on stones that danced

On stones that gave life

On stones that hold the imprint

Of Milarepa's foot

Holy foot trekking the paths

Of the stupas

The paths of holiness

The path of Dharma

We are we think we create we love we are

Holiness is cyclical

As is all life

Leading to wisdom

Thank You Music

I imagine listening to Beethoven
Brahms Bach Strauss Mahler Mozart
For the first time
Each moment an epiphany
Beyond perfection
Taking a journey with twists and turns
Noticing unexpected genius
For the first time
I grew up as a child with
Rachmaninoff and Rimski-Korsakov
As well as Brahms and Beethoven
My mother loved Offenbach
I grew up with music
And those friends continued to greet me
Through my whole life
But still surprise me with their genius
Other friends and muses
I got to know as a musician
Singing jazz with my brother
Himself a great jazz and classical pianist and composer
Stepped myself into the pond of composition
With my master pianist composer conductor first husband
And my lovely funk and jazz and classical pianist daughter
And my adored son who played and sang on stage as a child
In Wozzeck and a child in Carmen and Boheme
As did my beloved daughter, singing of a trumpet and a horse
At the Christmas market in the second act
And found music always holds and accepts
Always embraces
Always has room for one more child
In the glorious heaven
Of Bach Beethoven Brahms Puccini or Gershwin and Strayhorn
And all the family of angels
One more child to simply sit at their feet
And say thank you for music

A Pelican

A pelican stood tall

Among gulls

On a long arm

Reaching out from Pier 41

In San Francisco

Instead of looking alone

Bereft of his normal gang

Flying across the sky

He looked dignified and sovereign

Surveying the bay

Like a king

Among gulls

Perched inside Poetry

Sitting inside Shakespeare's words
I feel an intricate part of history
Involved in a historical dialogue
With ideas and ancient stories
Sitting inside Athenian words
I know Socrates asks questions and writes nothing
But is memorialized by Aristophanes
As a strange man in a basket
Speaking of the dangers of terrestrial water
Expounding on the mechanics of thunder
Curious and impatient
While Plato creates the wise
Questioning Socrates
Who probes youth to think
And pursues logic
In his arguments with accusers
Sitting inside Plato's discourse
I seek the wise Socrates
Who owed a cock to Asclepius
Leaving a riddle to further generations
With his last words
To continue the dialogue
Sitting inside Dante's words
I long to tag along
With him and Virgil
Just to listen to them
Discussing the journey
Of the human soul
Or perhaps consider
With other muses
The rigors of Milton's paradise

Lebanon

Lebanon
Birthplace of many gods
Where Cadmus sewed dragons' teeth
And raised warriors
Punished for killing the great dragon
Yet revered for the Phoenician alphabet
Built the great city of Tyre
Where a cow had led him as prophesied
Son of Phoenix
Father of Semele with Harmonia
Brother of Europa
Abducted by Zeus in the form of a bull
A scene made into music by Milhaud
She who gave birth to more gods
Lebanon
Birthplace of legends
Saturated with the blood of civil war
Exploited by fickle friends
A chaos of divinity and nature
Dragons and literacy
Home of a snail
Who bled purple for royalty
The die of kings
Deep rich purple
Color of coagulated blood
Said to make magic
For Lebanon
Country of mountains
Country of rivers and sea
Land of the Men of Sidon
Welcoming Phoenicians on their ships
Bringing trade and new ideas

To a Bronze Age people
5,000 years ago
Bringing Arabian Semites
Bringing Greek gods and goddesses
And bringing Roman conquest
By Alexander the Great
Leaving the country divided
With his death in 323 BCE
Yet strong under the Alexandrian legacy
Buddhist and Greek traditions thrived
Alongside Persian, Christian Muslim
Lebanon thrived with 18 religions
While Hellenism walked the streets of Lebanon
With the thoughts of Plato and Socrates
The Logos that permeated philosophies
Of ancient Phoenicians
And religions to come
Where wars were fought, empires crashed and arose
Fighting battles over this beauty of the Mediterranean
Once home to Nebuchadnezzar's hanging gardens
Home of Egyptian, Hittite, Assyrian, Ottoman
Considered the birthplace of civilization
On the Sumer river of Macedonia
Coveted still by modern western powers
Crouched over three fault lines
Suffered a vast earthquake and tsunami killing 30,000
Five hundred fifty years
After Jesus lived and died
Was baptized in 1943 as Lebanon, with Beirut as its capital
Beautiful Lebanon still suffers her plight of perfection
Long coastline and vast mountains
Loveliness and accessibility
Desired by all her neighbors
She must draw her skirts around her

And become her own mistress
Yet foreign powers do battle for her favors
Through the 1980's
Israel among her hostile suitors
Allows the massacre at Sabra Shatila
When 800 Palestinian refugees were killed
After being forced to leave Palestine for Lebanon
Only on paper an independent state
Her beauty smudged by those
Who will not leave her alone
Who assassinate her presidents
And massacre her refugees
Lebanon is trampled over even under UN protection
Her gardens turned to rubble through bombs
Her city now frightened again
With explosions on her pier
During the year of pandemic
She must cower in her own streets
Where history repeats its story of blood
Hanging gardens whisper of her past
Fault lines question her future
And the mountains and the sea
Remain her cradle
Rocking and singing
Over an ancient land

I am Palestine

I am Palestine
I live between the Mediterranean Sea and the Jordan River
My arms embrace Egypt, Syria and Arabia
I have born prophets and poets
Ishmael and Isaac
Sarah and Hagar
Humankind began in my womb
And seeded the world
Neanderthal children
Slept and dreamed
In my arms
Drank from the Wadi Natuf
Flowing past the west bank
Of their home
In the Shuqba cave
Burrowing deep
Into my ancestry
I am Palestine
My children
Lived and thought
In my arms
Thought and dreamed of tools
Stone and bronze
Observed the stars
Gave thanks
To the sun and the land
I am Palestine
Once I was a vassal to Egypt
My bronze artifacts
Bore tribute from Jerusalem's king
To Pharaoh
I am Palestine
My children have played with stone

And copper
Bronze and iron
Weapons made to forage
Were turned upon my children
And blood was shed
I am Palestine
I have seen much blood
As eras move to eras
I am Silwan
I am water
And fertile land
I am compassion
Neighbors of my children
Have been welcome
Ideas have been welcome
Edom, Ammon, and Moab
Ruled by King Sihon
Lived in peace
Within my arms
I am Palestine
My peace has shed my blood
Oh, tribe of Joseph from Qadesh
Why could you not live in peace
With Palestine?
I am Palestine
I see tribe upon tribe
Come to feast upon my land
Suckle at my breasts
And rape my peace
Foreign greed
Would make me pawn
To war
Crush my history
Break my bones

Feed them to my enemies
I am Palestine
I grow new bones
My children are murdered
Buried in rubble
Starved and imprisoned
By walls of stone and steel
And hatred
 I have seen stones and bronze and iron
Crushed in my arms
Buried in my soils
I am Palestine
I cannot be destroyed
My bones are made
Of angel dust
Angels' blood
Flows back into my veins
I am Palestine

Road to Al-Ja'una, Safad, Palestine
Ethnically cleansed in 1948

The Story of Lifta, a Palestinian Village

Yacoub was eight when Israel took away his home
When the soldiers expelled his family at gunpoint
He was eight when he last saw the grass and the yellow flowers
Blooming on cacti near the garden gate
Eight when soldiers began shooting at homes and families
While his mother was preparing a fire to warm the house
Eight when his father took him by the hand
And he and his eight siblings left everything behind to walk
across the valley
To walk to Ramallah
To walk to Jerusalem
To camp under trees until they could find shelter
Now decades later Jacoub climbs through weeds and tall grass
He climbs to the ruins of his home where he and his family lived
Where his mother baked bread in the taboun oven outside
Paradise he calls it
Where he played among almond and fig trees
Where he played on the rocks
Where he threw pebbles in the natural spring
Where he played and swam and bathed
Lifta, his village, where families helped each other with planting,
Helped each other with sewing and traditional embroidery
Where families raised their children together
Where they laughed and worked and played
Lifta is the only village left, for centuries prosperous and busy
Tucked into the northwest fringe of Jerusalem,
The only village not bulldozed over or covered with concrete and
tarmac
Or planted over with trees to make a park for orthodox Jews
Today Israel wants to turn the only remaining village over to
developers
To build luxury housing and a hotel
Israel wants to destroy Jakoub's home so he can never return

He still holds the key in his hand
A key that no longer fits the ruins of its doors
But a key that fits his heart
Here is my house, he says, though only the corners remain
This is my only real home, says Jacoub Odeh
Though his father died of a broken heart when he was 35
And his mother followed him soon after
And Jacoub spent 17 years in prison
Fighting for his home
He sees Jewish teenagers playing in the natural spring
Playing in the courtyard of his childhood village
Where he is not allowed
He knows hundreds of Palestinian villages have been destroyed
Some destroyed over and over again
As the people try always to rebuild, the seventh, eighth time
Until they can no longer remember how often they have rebuilt
their homes
And dared the bulldozers not to destroy them again
Only Lifta remains as ruins and memory of the Nakba, the
catastrophe for Palestinians
Government buildings, Houses of Parliament are planted on the
farmland
That belongs to Odeh and his village
Farmland where the soil grew olives, pomegranates,
Fig, apricot, almond, plum and citrus trees
Where the fields grew spinach, cauliflower, peas and beans
Where the spring watered all growing things
Making Lifta prosperous until 1948
The year 700,000 Palestinians were dispossessed
Of their homes and land
Since then waiting to go back
Waiting and returning
Always going back to rebuild
Jakoub gazes at the old mosque, the olive press, the cemetery

He gazes at the courtyard with the clear spring water
A courtyard built by the people of the village
The house where he and his father were born
Built by his grandparents and the people of the village
He sees them as they once were
Beautiful and welcoming
The people of the village do not want to see hotels
And luxury houses on their land
They do not want a UNESCO world heritage site
They do not want symbols of their loss
They do not want ruins to weep upon
They want to return home
To walk under the lintels etched in Arabic
"The owner of this house is god"

البــيت هو ال صاحب هذا

Lifta is an ancient city whose roots extend from the Iron Age to the Roman and Byzantine eras as well as the Ottoman Republic)